Antigua

DIRECTIONS

REDCLIFFE STREET

WRITTEN AND RESEARCHED BY

Adam Vaitilingam

and

Romesh Vaitilingam

D1417244

ROUGH GUIDES

NEW YORK • LONDON • DELHI
www.roughguides.com

Contents

Introduction to

Antigua

Little known just a generation ago, tiny Antigua has established itself as one of the Caribbean's more popular destinations. The island is dotted with superb stretches of white sand, many of which – despite the upswing in tourism and development that has given birth to dozens of excellent restaurants and hotels, and a handful of all-inclusives – remain relatively uncrowded. If you're looking for a place to crash out on a beach for a week or two, you'll find this laid-back, welcoming place hard to beat.

The best of the beaches can be found at Dickenson Bay in the northwest, Half Moon Bay in the east and Rendezvous Bay in the south. Of these, only Dickenson Bay (along with its neighbour, Runaway Bay) are part of a major tourist strip; the others – as well as several more just

like them – are much less built up than similarly idyllic spots in the

When to visit

For many visitors, Antigua's leading attraction is its **tropical climate**: hot and sunny all year round. The weather is at its best from mid-December to mid-April, with rainfall low and the heat tempered by cooling trade winds. Things can get noticeably hotter during the summer and, particularly in September and October, the humidity can become oppressive. September is also the most threatening month of the annual hurricane season, which runs officially from June 1 to October 31.

▲ Dickenson Bay

Caribbean. The waters off the north coast are also a prime spot for spray-soaked watersports, with excellent scuba diving and snorkelling opportunities in the fabulous offshore reefs.

Before Europeans began colonizing the West Indies, Antigua was populated by Arawak-speaking Amerindians. Sighted by Columbus in 1493, the island was left to its own devices until the early six-teenth century, when British settlers arrived, bringing with them African slaves to clear the native vegetation and plant sugarcane. For centuries, the island was little more than a giant sugar factory, producing sugar and rum to send home to an increasingly sweet-toothed mother country. Around Antigua, the tall brick chimneys of a hundred deserted and decaying sugar mills, as well as the ruins of military forts and signal stations, bear witness to that long colonial era.

These relics make for worthy and atmospheric diversions if you can drag yourself away from your patch of sand. The superbly restored naval dockyard and the crumbling forts around English Harbour and Shirley Heights are as impressive as any historic site in the West Indies. There are lots of other lit-tle nuggets to explore too, including the capital, St John's, with its colourful, lively quayside, and the odd old-fashioned settle-

◀ Steel bands play at Shirley Heights

ment like Parham or Old Road that progress seems to have bypassed. And if you're prepared to do a bit of walking, you'll find some superb hikes that will take you out to completely isolated parts of the island. As for nightlife, things are generally pretty quiet, though a good crop of restaurants – look out for those serving fresh West Indian cooking, especially seafood – do double duty as bars and dance clubs.

Meanwhile, Antigua's sister island **Barbuda** feels a world apart from its larger, more-developed neighbour, even though it's just

fifteen minutes away by plane. With its spectacular, largely deserted beaches and pristine coral reefs, it may come as some surprise that tourism here is as low-key as it is – which is all the more reason to visit.

▲ A snack shop in Liberta

>> **ANTIGUA** AT A GLANCE

◄ St John's

St John's

Tucked into an inlet on the northwest coast, St John's most likely won't be why you come to Antigua, but to miss out on the city's great restaurants, entertaining commercial quays and vibrant daily life would be a shame. Be sure also to check out the cathedral, the cricket ground and the national museum.

The northwest coast

Just north of St John's, Antigua's northwest coast holds two well-manicured tourist areas: quiet Runaway Bay and more-developed Dickenson Bay. Both offer lovely beaches, shelving gently down into turquoise waters – visit Runaway for relaxed swimming, and Dickenson for fun watersports.

The Atlantic coast

The underdeveloped Atlantic coast is Antigua at its most wild and natural state: deserted islands, abandoned sugar plantations and a lengthy stretch of rough, but incredibly scenic, coastline are all big draws for those willing to explore off the beaten track.

◄ Dickenson Bay

8

Falmouth and English Harbour

Falmouth and English Harbour

Though not much for good beaches, Falmouth and English Harbour contain most of the island's top sights. The nicely restored Nelson's Dockyard is a clear window to Antigua's colonial past, while the barbecue parties on Shirley Heights keep things jumping.

The west coast

Antigua's west coast is the island's major tourist area. Highlights include Darkwood Beach, great for snorkelling and beachcombing; the massive Jolly Harbour resort and entertainment complex; and a hike up 400-metre Boggy Peak, the island's highest point.

Abandoned west coast sugarcane mill

Barbuda

Forty-eight kilometres north of Antigua, the island of Barbuda is perfect for those seeking unspoilt nature. It's likely you won't see a soul lounging with you on the beaches, scuba diving the coral reefs or viewing the colony of frigate birds.

Redonda

Near-impossible to reach, Redonda is a small chunk of volcanic rock populated only by goats and seabirds. Still, the story of how it came to be claimed as an independent kingdom is delightfully weird; see p.106 for more.

Ideas

The big six

There are a handful of places on Antigua that will give you a fully rounded picture of the country's rich **colonial history** – in essence the best of what's worth seeing beyond the countless beaches. A comprehensive tour takes you all around the island, from the capital city to the ruins around Falmouth and English Harbour to the rolling countryside along the island's Atlantic coast. To complete your impression, it's worth hanging around for either of the two main **festivals** that help define the nation in the eyes of the world.

Nelson's Dockyard

Nelson called Antigua "this infernal hole", but his name has been borrowed for this beautifully restored and quite unmissable Georgian dockyard.

▶P.74 ▶ FALMOUTH AND ENGLISH HARBOUR

Shirley Heights

A visit to the Heights offers the chance not only to explore military history but also to get some wonderful views and, on Sunday, to party at *The Lookout*.

▶P.78 ▶ FALMOUTH AND ENGLISH HARBOUR

St John's Cathedral

Viewed from the ocean, the Baroque twin towers dominate the skyline of the capital, earning its reputation as the most imposing of all West Indian cathedrals.

▸P.43 ▸ ST JOHN'S ▲

Carnival

Beginning in late July, Antigua – St John's especially – is consumed by Carnival, which sees a week and a half of non stop music and dance, culminating in a spectacular costume parade.

▸P.40 ▸ ST JOHN'S ▲

Sailing Week

One of the world's premier sailing events, attracting mariners from across the globe – but you don't have to be a yachtie to enjoy the party.

▸P.76 ▸ FALMOUTH AND ENGLISH HARBOUR ▼

Betty's Hope

The island's most prominent sugar plantation for more than two hundred years and now the only working sugar mill in the Caribbean.

▸P.64 ▸ THE ATLANTIC COAST ▼

Beaches

Most visitors to Antigua head straight for the **beach** and, as a result, the most popular ones can get especially packed out. While the west and northwest coasts see calmer seas, the winds and frequent swells on the Atlantic coast make for great bodysurfing, windsurfing and, for the really energetic, kiteboarding. Several strips also have great options for lunch on the beach, notably the superb west-coast stretch that takes in Darkwood Beach, Crabbe Hill Beach and Turner's Beach.

Dickenson Bay

A beautiful half-mile stretch of white powder sand and calm waters offering a fine choice of hotels, restaurants and watersports.

▸P.54 ▸ THE NORTHWEST COAST

Darkwood Beach

A wonderfully quiet stretch on the west coast, featuring views across to Montserrat and, in nearby *OJs*, probably Antigua's best beach bar.

▸P91 ▸ THE WEST COAST

Green Island

Take a boat ride out from Harmony Hall and find your very own strip of sand on this peaceful and uninhabited island.

▶P.66 ▶ THE ATLANTIC COAST ▼

Pigeon Beach

The best beach in the area around Falmouth and English Harbour, especially good for snorkelling and simply kicking back with a book.

▶P.78 ▶ FALMOUTH AND ENGLISH HARBOUR ▲

Rendezvous Bay

One of the most remote beaches on the island, but well worth hiking in for the fine white sand, the calm waters and the solitude.

▶P.71 ▶ FALMOUTH AND ENGLISH HARBOUR ▲

Half Moon Bay

This beautiful crescent bay must be a contender for one of the best beaches in the Caribbean, if not the world.

▶P.66 ▶ THE ATLANTIC COAST ▲

Restaurants

Antigua has a growing selection of top-quality **restaurants**, showcasing great chefs and cuisine from around the world, as well as superb **local ingredients**, particularly those freshly pulled from the ocean. Most of the classy places are away from the big hotels and all-inclusives, but it's well worth getting out to them. You can also enjoy great food at local spots like *Hemingway's* and *George* in St John's, and *Caribbean Taste* and *Jackee's Kwik Stop* around Falmouth and English Harbour.

Coconut Grove

Romantic open-air thatched restaurant on the water's edge at the *Siboney Beach Club*, known for its sensational seafood.

▶P.58 ▶ THE NORTHWEST COAST ▼

Bay House

A lovely terrace location high in the hills above Dickenson Bay, with dependably excellent food and service.

▶P.57 ▶ THE NORTHWEST COAST ▼

Julian's Alfresco

Runaway Bay is a quiet part of the island, but worth visiting for Julian Waterer's outstanding cuisine served in a delightful beachside garden.

▸P.58 ▸ THE NORTHWEST COAST ▲

Home

Chef Carl Thomas's childhood home on the outskirts of St John's, where he and his German wife Rita now serve first-rate West Indian food.

▸P.48 ▸ ST JOHN'S ▼

Harmony Hall

The perfect spot for a long Italian lunch, perhaps taking a couple of hours' beach break on nearby Green Island before dessert and coffee.

▸P.68 ▸ THE ATLANTIC COAST ▼

Sheer

With a magnificent cliff-top location and a menu of Asian/South American fusion, this *Cocobay Resort* restaurant compares with anything you'll find in New York or London.

▸P.97 ▸ THE WEST COAST ▲

Colonial forts

The British, who ruled Antigua for over three centuries, left behind numerous **military fortifications**. Many were first built when the British and French navies were contesting the islands of the Caribbean in the 1660s and several were enlarged or strengthened during the Napoleonic wars. They must have been an effective deterrent since they never saw any further action, instead becoming signal stations, reporting on the movement of ships in the vicinity. Most are now pretty dilapidated, though they all still command great views.

Fort James

Just north of St John's, Fort James is one of the island's best-preserved military installations. It's also right near the popular Fort Bay beach.

▸P.51 ▸ THE NORTHWEST COAST ▲

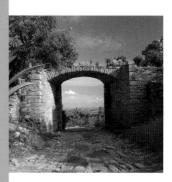

Great Fort George

Extensive ruins high in the hills above Falmouth and English Harbour; you'll only make it up here on foot or by four-wheel-drive.

▸P.73 ▸ FALMOUTH AND ENGLISH
HARBOUR ▲

Fort Berkeley

Atmospheric ruins at the mouth of English Harbour, just a short stroll from Nelson's Dockyard.

▸P.76 ▸ FALMOUTH AND ENGLISH HARBOUR ▾

Dow's Hill Fort

These rather limited ruins are in a superb location high above English Harbour, with a small multimedia museum nearby that neatly summarizes the island's history.

▸P.79 ▸ FALMOUTH AND ENGLISH HARBOUR ▾

Corbison Point

A tiny bit of eighteenth-century military history on the spit of land between Dickenson Bay and Runaway Bay.

▸P.53 ▸ THE NORTHWEST COAST ▲

On the water

The waters around Antigua are invariably clean, crystal-clear and warm; besides lapping around in them, you'll find them well suited for a wide variety of **watersports**. Just offshore, you can choose to cruise, sail, kayak, snorkel, bodysurf, windsurf, kiteboard, waterski, jetski or swim with dolphins and stingrays. Further out, you could try some deep-sea sport fishing, going after wahoo, tuna, marlin and other sailfish. Underwater, there are some spectacular dive sites, with coral canyons, caves, walls and shipwrecks, home to all kinds of tropical fish and other marine creatures.

Boating with Wadadli Cats

Catamaran cruises are a great way to explore the island, snorkel some of the offshore reefs or simply relax with a rum punch.

▶ P.120 ▶ ESSENTIALS ▲

Windsurfing on Dickenson Bay

One of the busiest strips of beach on the island, but the wind and waters are perfect for windsurfers, whether you're experienced or just starting out.

▸P.54 ▸ THE NORTHWEST COAST ▼

Kiteboarding at Jabberwock Beach

Try this spectacular new sport if you dare: KiteAntigua has introduced it to a windswept beach on the island's Atlantic coast.

▸P.60 ▸ THE ATLANTIC COAST ▲

Sailing with Sunsail Club Colonna

Sunsail has the best equipment and the best location for dinghy sailing – particularly good for getting kids out on the water.

▸P.68 ▸ THE ATLANTIC COAST ▼

Kayaking eco-tours

Explore the island's hidden reefs, inlets and mangrove swamps by kayak with Eli Fuller's Adventure Antigua or "Paddles" Kayak & Snorkel Club.

▸P.120 ▸ ESSENTIALS ▲

Antiguan specialities

You can find well-prepared versions of most of the big international cuisines on Antigua, but make sure you also try some of the **local specialities**. Fresh seafood and exotic fruit and vegetables are in abundance, and it's worth tasting them cooked up in traditional West Indian style. Look out, too, for the national fruit, the succulently sweet Antiguan black pineapple, as well as delicious local dishes like ducana, fungi, souse and a variety of curries. For **drinking**, local beer and rum-based cocktails are the best options.

Rum

Antiguan rums include the English Harbour and Cavalier brands; the best place to pick up a bottle is in any of the beautiful old Long Street liquor stores.

▶ P49 ▶ ST JOHN'S ▼

Wadadli beer

The Carib Indians called the island Wadadli, now the name of the local brew.

▶P.117 ▶ ESSENTIALS ▲

Market fish

Freshly caught fish is often the best menu option, with snapper and jack in particularly plentiful supply.

▶P.45 ▶ ST JOHN'S ▼

Pepperpot stew

Made with salt beef, pumpkin and okra, this is a favourite dish in homes across the Caribbean.

▶P.85 ▶ FALMOUTH AND ENGLISH HARBOUR ▲

Fresh fruit and vegetables

The public market in St John's is one of the best places for sampling some of the island's exotic fruit and vegetables.

▶P.45 ▶ ST JOHN'S ▼

Museums and galleries

A handful of small **museums** around the island neatly pull together Antigua's history. You'll find fascinating perspectives on the pre-Columbian period, the early European settlers and the boom years of British colonialism, dominated here by the sugar industry and the slave trade, and followed by emancipation and the road to national independence. There are also several excellent **galleries**, showcasing the work of artists and craftsmen from Antigua and elsewhere in the Caribbean.

National Museum of Antigua and Barbuda

A lovingly assembled collection of exhibits on the island's past and present, from Arawak artifacts to a famous cricket bat.

▶ P.41 ▶ ST JOHN'S ▲

Betty's Hope

The museum at this restored sugar mill recalls, through various tools and drawings, the time when sugar was king – and is a sobering reminder of the slave trade that made this possible.

▶ P.64 ▶ THE ATLANTIC COAST ▲

Nelson's Dockyard Museum

The world's only working Georgian dock-yard includes a maritime museum that recounts the story of English Harbour.

▶ P.75 ▶ FALMOUTH AND ENGLISH HARBOUR ▼

Heavenly Hill Art Gallery

Terrence Sprague's gallery may have moved from the west coast to Nelson's Dockyard, but it retains its reputation for promoting original work by local artists.

▶ P.76 ▶ FALMOUTH AND ENGLISH HARBOUR ▲

Nick Maley's Island Arts Gallery

Meet the creator of the *Star Wars* character Yoda at his downtown St John's gallery, close to where the cruise ships come in.

▶ P.39 ▶ ST JOHN'S ▼

Harmony Hall

The gallery at this restored plantation house (and outstanding Italian restaurant) shows art by top Caribbean artists and sculptors.

▶ P.66 ▶ THE ATLANTIC COAST ▲

Hikes

Dragging yourself away from the sand and sea won't be easy during your stay, but there are plenty of outdoor activities waiting if you do. **Hiking** is one of the most enjoyable of these: there are several great routes you can try, with varying degrees of difficulty and the choice of whether you want to go with a guide. Many of the most frequented tracks and trails lead to various hilltops and fortifications, where you can reflect back on the road you travelled. Others take you to beautiful beaches with few if any people around – the flip side of the Antigua most visitors see.

Falmouth to Rendezvous Bay

It's about an hour's hike from Falmouth to the idyllic beach at Rendezvous Bay, or you can take the scenic route down through the woodlands from Fig Tree Drive.

▸ P.73 ▸ FALMOUTH AND ENGLISH HARBOUR ▾

Wallings Woodlands

This forest reserve features some delightful nature trails – look out for mangoes, hog plums, passion fruit and lemongrass.

▶P.90 ▶ THE WEST COAST ▼

Middle Ground

West of Nelson's Dockyard, you can hike up onto this unusual peninsula for great views back across Falmouth and English Harbour.

▶P.77 ▶ FALMOUTH AND ENGLISH HARBOUR ▲

Boggy Peak

The communication station rather spoils the view of Boggy Peak, but the view back down certainly justifies hiking up to the highest point on the island.

▶P91 ▶ THE WEST COAST ▼

Indian Creek

Look out over Eric Clapton's house and spectacular Willoughby Bay as you scramble steeply downhill to the creek.

▶P.80 ▶ FALMOUTH AND ENGLISH HARBOUR ▲

Entertainment and nightilfe

You'll easily find ready-made evening **entertainment** at the big resort hotels. But if you want to be a little more adventurous, there's plenty of non-pre-packaged **fun** to be had, especially around Falmouth and English Harbour. Try your luck at the gaming tables, get up and dance at various restaurants-cum-nightclubs or party with the locals to the latest Caribbean sounds. None of it may be particularly cutting-edge, but preceded by a few cocktails on the beach should be all the excitement you need.

Abracadabra

A great place at English Harbour for southern Italian food – and once you've finished eating, a great place to hit the dance floor for R&B and Eighties dance music.

▸ P.83 ▸ FALMOUTH AND ENGLISH HARBOUR ▲

The Sticky Wicket

Next to the brand-new Stanford Cricket Ground, you can watch the national pastime day or night, live or on TV, in a convivial setting.

▸ P.69 ▸ THE ATLANTIC COAST ▲

The Lookout

Sunday is party time up on Shirley Heights, when crowds of locals and visitors gather to enjoy reggae and steel bands.

▸ P.85 ▸ FALMOUTH AND ENGLISH HARBOUR ▲

Life

Perched on a wooden pier right across the street from *Abracadabra*, this place has just as much action, but with a Sixties and Seventies musical bent.

▸ P.85 ▸ FALMOUTH AND ENGLISH HARBOUR ▲

Rush nightclub and Grand Princess Casino

At the Jolly Harbour entertainment complex, this is the newest and most popular nightspot on the island, with facilities for the casino enthusiast, too.

▸ P.98 ▸ THE WEST COAST ▲

Great views

Beyond the sunshine, the year-round warm temperatures and the fabulous beaches, Antigua is blessed with many other exquisite natural phenomena, including lush tropical vegetation, dramatic rock formations and some choice lookout points to get a panoramic **view** of the island. Make it a priority to explore some of these splendid sights, perhaps by renting a car for a day or two, asking a taxi driver to give you a full tour or taking an organized excursion to the high spots of the island's interior.

Fig Tree Drive

This drive through the most lushly forested part of the island offers some great views but no figs: it's the Antiguan word for bananas.

▸ P.88 ▸ THE WEST COAST ▾

Devil's Bridge

Over the centuries, Atlantic breakers have carved a natural limestone arch and blowholes where surf crashes up and through.

▸ P.65 ▸ THE ATLANTIC COAST ▾

Hawksbill Rock

About half a mile offshore, this huge rock bears a striking resemblance to the head of a hawksbill turtle, the most endangered species of sea turtle.

▶ P.93 ▶ THE WEST COAST ◀

Shirley Heights

The best place on the island to watch the sunset, whether or not you get to see the legendary "green flash".

▶ P.78 ▶ FALMOUTH AND ENGLISH HARBOUR ▶

Fort Berkeley

A superb vantage point for viewing some of the world's finest yachts under sail during Sailing Week.

▶ P.76 ▶ FALMOUTH AND ENGLISH HARBOUR ▼

Fort Barrington

Across St John's harbour from Fort James, this beautiful but isolated spot is better known by locals as Goat Hill.

▶ P.93 ▶ THE WEST COAST ▼

Barbuda

Just 48 kilometres north of Antigua lies **Barbuda**, the nation's other inhabited island. Chief among its attractions are the stunning and often deserted white-sand beaches, but it's also a great place for scuba diving and birdwatching, notably for a rare colony of frigate birds. The island has a colourful history, particularly during its two hundred years of ownership by the Codrington family. But you'll really want to come here to get away from it all: Barbuda is close to being the ultimate Caribbean escape.

Frigate bird sanctuary

The Caribbean's largest nesting colony of these fabulous and unusual birds is a must for twitchers.

▸ P.102 ▸ BARBUDA ▲

Spanish Point

There's little evidence of things Spanish on this southeastern tip of the island, but a spectacular marine reserve – Palaster Reef – lies just offshore.

▸ P106 ▸ BARBUDA ▲

Palm Beach

An absolute dream of a beach, which, more often than not, you can have to yourself.

▶ P.103 ▶ BARBUDA

Martello tower

Once the heart of the island's defences and still a great lookout spot to survey the island and surrounding ocean.

▶ P.105 ▶ BARBUDA

Caves

Take a break from the beach to explore the caves in Barbuda's Highlands, several of which are decorated with ancient carvings.

▶ P.104 ▶ BARBUDA

K Club

Enjoy the height of luxury, even if you're only there for lunch, at Barbuda's star hotel, which gets its K from the famous Italian designer Krizia.

▶ P.107 ▶ BARBUDA

Places

Places

St John's

With a population of around 30,000 – nearly half the island's total – bustling **St John's** is Antigua's capital and only city. No one could claim it's the prettiest town in the West Indies, but it does have a certain immediate charm. In the city centre, there are plenty of attractive old wooden and stone buildings – some of them superbly renovated, others in a perilous state of near-collapse – among the less appealing modern developments. It'll only take you a couple of hours to see everything, but, even if you're not staying in the capital, you'll probably want to come back for at least one evening to sample some of the city's excellent restaurants.

While in town, don't miss Redcliffe Quay – where the waterfront and its colonial buildings have been attractively restored – or the tiny National Museum, which offers a well-presented rundown on the country's history and culture. If you've got time, take a stroll through some of the old streets and check out the city's twin-towered cathedral, perched on top of Newgate Street. As for where to eat, drink and shop for souvenirs, Redcliffe Quay and nearby Heritage Quay are your best bets – though you'll probably want to avoid these areas if the cruise ships are in, when the steel drums come out to play "Feeling Hot, Hot, Hot" and the area almost disappears beneath a scrum of duty-free shoppers.

▼ ST JOHN'S HARBOUR

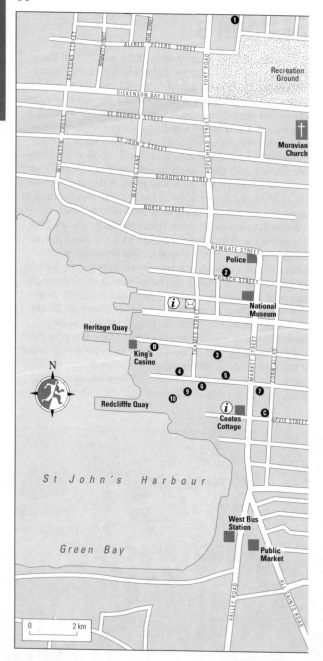

1

ALFRED PETERS STREET
GRAYSONS STREET
BENNETT STREET
MICHAEL STREET
FORT ROAD

Recreation
Ground

DICKENSON BAY STREET

ST. GEORGES STREET
POPESHEAD STREET

ST. JOHN'S STREET

WILKINSON CROSS

†
Moravian
Church

WAPER LANE

BISHOPGATE STREET

NORTH STREET

NEWGATE STREET
Police

2
CHURCH STREET

ℹ ✉

**National
Museum**

THAMES STREET

Heritage Quay

**Ⓑ
King's
Casino**

3

MARKET STREET

4

5

6

CORN ALLEY

7

9

10

Redcliffe Quay

ℹ
**Coates
Cottage**

Ⓒ

NEVIS STREET

N

St John's Harbour

Green Bay

**West Bus
Station**

**Public
Market**

VALLEY ROAD
ALL SAINTS ROAD

0   2 km

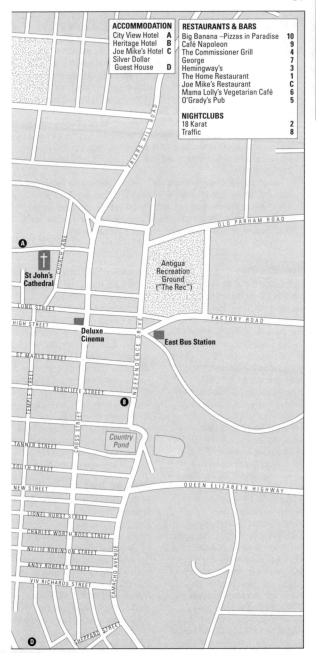

ACCOMMODATION
City View Hotel	A
Heritage Hotel	B
Joe Mike's Hotel	C
Silver Dollar Guest House	D

RESTAURANTS & BARS
Big Banana –Pizzas in Paradise	10
Café Napoleon	9
The Commissioner Grill	4
George	7
Hemingway's	3
The Home Restaurant	1
Joe Mike's Restaurant	C
Mama Lolly's Vegetarian Café	6
O'Grady's Pub	5

NIGHTCLUBS
| 18 Karat | 2 |
| Traffic | 8 |

St John's Cathedral

Antigua Recreation Ground ("The Rec.")

Deluxe Cinema

East Bus Station

Country Pond

FRIARS HILL ROAD

CHURCH LANE

OLD PARHAM ROAD

LONG STREET

HIGH STREET

FACTORY ROAD

ST MARYS STREET

INDEPENDENCE DRIVE

REDCLIFFE STREET

TEMPLE STREET

CROSS STREET

TANNER STREET

SOUTH STREET

NEW STREET

QUEEN ELIZABETH HIGHWAY

LIONEL HURST STREET

CHARLES WORTH ROSS STREET

NELLIE ROBINSON STREET

ANDY ROBERTS STREET

VIV RICHARDS STREET

CAMACHO AVENUE

SHEPPARD STREET

St John's **PLACES**

As all of the main places of interest in St John's are close together, the easiest way to see the city is **on foot**. If you'd rather use your car, be advised that **driving** around town is straightforward if not particularly enjoyable; parking space is limited, the one-way traffic system a little tricky to deal with, and potholes and roadside rain gullies threaten damage to your car at every turn. There are **taxi** stands just west of the market at the southern end of town, beside the east bus station near the Antigua Recreation Ground, and at Heritage Quay.

If you're arriving in or leaving the city by **bus**, keep in mind that the east bus station serves the north (Dickenson Bay, Cedar Grove and the airport) and the east (Parham and Willikies) of the island, while the west bus station, next to the market, serves the west (Five Islands) and south (Jolly Harbour, Old Road, Falmouth and English Harbour).

The government's main **tourist office**, at the western end of Nevis Street (Mon–Sat 9am–5pm; ☎ 462 0480, ⊛ www.antigua-barbuda.org), has a perfunctory smattering of island brochures; they also give out free road maps. For more practical information about any big **events** going on while you're in town, you'll need to rely on flyers, the newspaper, radio ads and word of mouth.

Redcliffe Quay

By the waterside at the western end of Redcliffe Street. Redcliffe Quay is the best place to start your tour of the city. Named in honour of the church of St Mary Redcliffe in the English port city of Bristol, this is one of the oldest parts of St John's, and incorporates many old warehouses – now attractively restored as small boutiques, restaurants and bars – and a wooden boardwalk that runs alongside the water. There's not a whole lot to see, but these several acres are a pleasant place to wander and soak up some of the city's history.

Many of the waterfront warehouses here once held supplies for the British navy and local merchant ships that traded between Antigua and the mother country during the eighteenth century – barrels of sugar and rum, lumber for ship repairs, cotton and sheepskins. The area behind the quay around the western end of Nevis Street held a number of barracoons, compounds where slaves were held after they arrived on the island and before they were sent off to the plantations or shipped on to other Caribbean islands.

Built on the side of one such barracoon is the recently restored **Coates Cottage**. When the owner of the house is present, he is happy for you to wander through to the small walled courtyard where the slaves were once held. The adjacent wooden building used to be a bargaining house, where auctions were held and slaves sold off to local estate-owners.

Heritage Quay

By the waterside at the western end of St Mary's Street. This modern concrete quay is given over to cruise-ship arrivals and dozens of duty-free shops designed to catch the tourist dollars, along with a purpose-built mall where local vendors flog T-shirts and distinctive Haitian art. Unless you're shopping or heading to the King's Casino (see opposite), there's little reason to stop by except for a quick look at the

▲ HERITAGE QUAY

Island Arts Gallery

Heritage Quay ☎462 2787, ⓦwww.yodaguy.com. Mon–Sat 10am–6pm. This is probably the most noteworthy of all the stores at Heritage Quay. The owner, British painter Nick Maley, was originally a film make-up artist who worked on movies such as *Star Wars* (for which he created the Yoda character). Today, he's lived on Antigua for nearly twenty years, showing his striking and original works at exhibitions across the Caribbean and North America. The small gallery here is crammed with Maley's paintings and prints, as well as those of Antiguan, Haitian and other West Indian artists. Though the artists are mostly little-known outside their home islands, there is plenty of exuberant colour and some captivating local portraits beside the more predictable land- and seascapes.

Long Street

Long Street is home to most of the party action during the ten-day Carnival each July and August (see box, overleaf). The street holds many of St John's finest old buildings, including a couple of fabulously colourful liquor stores, still in business after more than a century (see "Shops", p.49).

The Rec

Eastern end of Long Street. Modest and unassuming as it looks, the Rec is one of the finest cricket pitches in the Caribbean. Blessed by low rainfall and year-round sun, and with its outfield and wicket lovingly tended by trusted inmates from the nearby prison, it looks at quiet times like any cricket pitch in England or Australia.

Westerby Memorial Fountain, which commemorates a Moravian missionary dedicated to helping Antiguans in the decades after emancipation from slavery in 1834, and to visit the Island Arts Gallery.

King's Casino

Heritage Quay ☎462 1727, ⓦwww.kingscasino.com, ⓔinfo@kingscasino.com. Mon–Sat 10am–4am, Sun 6pm–4am. The city's main casino, packed with slot machines and offering blackjack, roulette and Caribbean stud poker tables for the more serious players. Live bands and karaoke give the place a bit of atmosphere after 10pm. The casino will normally lay on one-way shuttle services to St John's for those coming to gamble for the night. It'll pick you up anywhere, but you'll be stuck with the taxi fare home – so make sure to win big.

▲ CLAPBOARD HOUSE

Don't believe it for a moment. On match days, while the rest of the island comes to a standstill, the ground is transformed into a cacophonous whirligig, with music belting from the stands, hordes of vendors flogging jerk chicken and Red Stripe, men on stilts and women in wigs.

If you've got any sense of adventure, head for Chickie's

Carnival

The highlight of Antigua's entertainment calendar is **Carnival**, an action-packed ten-day party held from late July until the first Tuesday in August. Warm-ups start in early July, with steel bands, Calypsonians and DJs in action across the island, while Carnival proper gets cracking with the opening of Carnival City at the Rec (see overleaf). This is where all of the scheduled events take place, though you'll often find spontaneous outbreaks of partying across the city. A festival village is set up nearby to provide space for the masses of food and drink vendors who emerge out of nowhere.

The major Carnival events take place over the last weekend, when you'll feel compelled to forgo sleep for a few days of frantic action. The Panorama steel band contest (Friday night) and the Calypso Monarch competition (Sunday night) are both packed and definitely worth catching, while on Monday morning – the day on which the islands celebrate slave emancipation in 1834 – Jouvert (pronounced "jouvay," and meaning daybreak) is a huge jump-up party starting at 4am. The Judging of the Troupes and Groups competition in the afternoon sees ranks of brightly costumed marching bands and floats parading through the city streets, being marked for colour, sound and general party attitude.

On Tuesday there's a final costumed parade through the streets, finishing with the announcement of all of the winners and a roughly 6pm–midnight last lap from Carnival City – "the bacchanal" – as the exhausted partygoers stream through St John's, led by the steel bands. All in all, it's a excellent event: certainly one of the best of the Caribbean's summer carnivals, and a great chance to catch Antiguans

Cricket in Antigua

If you're in Antigua for any length of time, you'll find it almost impossible to avoid the subject of **cricket** – the true national passion. If you're lucky, there'll be a game at the Rec during your stay; if so, don't miss the chance to get along and check out the calypso atmosphere. Failing that, expect at least to get roped into a game of beach cricket, where you'll find fielders standing under the palm trees and in the sea waiting for a miscued shot.

Cricket arrived in Antigua via the British military in the mid-nineteenth century. The 59th Foot Regiment formed the island's first club on New Year's Day 1842, and the *Antigua Times* recorded an Antigua XI beaten by the crew of the HMS *Phaeton* at Shirley Heights on September 26, 1863. For decades, cricket clubs remained the preserve of the ruling class: strictly whites-only and often little more than extended social clubs for the planters and merchants. But, despite the early snobbery that was attached to the game, it soon began to catch on in the sugar estates, where the workers drew up their own pitches and organized matches.

In 1895 Antigua received its first overseas touring team, who reported playing against a home team composed entirely of "coloured" players. (On the same tour, by comparison, the authorities in Barbados excluded black players from their team, irrespective of merit.) In 1920 the Rising Sun Cricket Club was founded for poor men in St John's, and by the 1930s – half a century before independence – Antigua had its first black sporting hero in the batsman **Pat Nanton**.

Nonetheless, Antigua remained a cricketing minnow well into the twentieth century, with the regional game dominated by the "Big Four" cricket nations: Jamaica, Barbados, Trinidad and Guyana. In 1966 the Caribbean Shell Shield competition was established for those four and a fifth team – the Combined Islands – made up of players from Antigua and the other small islands. Rarely taken seriously during the 1970s, this Combined Islands team swept to victory in the Shield in 1981, the year of Antigua's independence, led by the brilliant Antiguan **Viv Richards** (see box, p.43). From that time, the Combined Islands team was allowed to become two – the Leeward Islands of the northeastern Caribbean (dominated by Antigua) and the Windward Islands of the southeast (including Grenada, St Vincent and St Lucia) – with the Leewards team consistently performing well in both the Shield and the one-day Red Stripe Cup, inaugurated in 1982.

Double Decker stand at the north end of the ground. With his banks of huge speakers tied to the railings, the eponymous DJ blasts everyone within earshot with the songs of local Calypsonians, and they all sing along to the chorus of "Rally Round the West Indies". Bumping and grinding away, more intent on the beer and the chat-up lines than the cricket, the happy spectators will be there long after stumps have been drawn and the players have retired to the pavilion.

The National Museum

Corner of Long and Market streets. Mon–Fri 8.30am–4pm, Sat 10am–2pm. Free. Housed in a 1747 Neoclassical courthouse, the National Museum of Antigua and Barbuda occupies just one large room, but it's indisputably worth thirty minutes of your time while you're exploring the capital – you can almost feel the enthusiasm with which the collection has been assembled and displayed. The exhibits start by showing off the islands' early geological history, backed up by fossils and coral skeletons, and move on to more extensive coverage of their first, Amerindian inhabitants. Jewellery, primitive tools, pottery shards and religious figures used by these early settlers have been found at sites across Antigua and Barbuda and are well laid out here, with brief descriptions of their significance.

The museum has small displays on Columbus, the European invasion and sugar production. An interesting 1750 map of Antigua shows the plantations, as well as all the reefs that threatened shipping around the island. There is also an unusual exhibit on the emancipation of the slaves and the resulting patterns of settlement. Upon emancipation in 1834 there were only four towns on Antigua, with almost all the ex-slaves living on the sugar estates; the planters usually refused to sell them land, since they wanted to keep them tied to the plantations. The exhibit shows how – either with the assistance of missionaries or by sheer determination – the former slaves were able to set themselves up in "free villages" across the island.

Elsewhere, there are displays on the island of **Barbuda**, which might whet your appetite for a visit (see p.100), and the tiny uninhabited rock of **Redonda** (see p.106). There's also an example of the ancient game of *warri* or *mancala*, brought by slaves from Africa's Gold Coast, and, rather bizarrely, a rhinoceros skull from Rwanda. Last but certainly not least, one of the museum's most prized exhibits is the cricket bat with which, in 1986, Antiguan Vivian Richards (now Sir Vivian) scored the fastest-ever test-match century, taking just 56 balls to score 100 runs against England on his home turf (see box, opposite).

Once you've finished your tour, take a peek in the small gift shop, where you can pick up pottery, reproduction maps of the islands, postcards and books.

▼ THE NATIONAL MUSEUM

Vivi and other Antiguan cricketing heroes

The first Antiguan to play for the West Indies team was fast bowler Andy Roberts, who made his debut against England in 1974; he was shortly followed by Vivian Richards, who first played against India in the same year. Within a couple of years both players had made a dramatic impact on the side – heavily involved in the slaughter of English cricket in 1976 – and in 1981 the island was awarded the right to stage its first test match, where Richards made the superb century discussed in the National Museum account (see opposite).

It's hard to overestimate the importance of Vivi (as he's known locally) to the development of the country's self-confidence in the years immediately before and after independence in 1981. For this tiny island to have produced a man rated by many as the finest batsman of his generation was an enormous boost to its self-esteem. Throughout his career, Richards's spectacular hitting and imperious manner endeared him to a generation of cricket-watchers worldwide. Now retired, Richards has eschewed the political career many expected, but the street where he was born in St John's now bears his name (it runs east–west just south of the public market) and – as a "goodwill ambassador" – he remains one of Antigua's most precious living assets.

Though unthinkable just two decades ago, today tiny Antigua is one of the leading cricketing venues in the Caribbean, with test matches, Busta Cup and Red Stripe Cup games played there annually. Between 1985 and 1995 the West Indies team was captained by Antiguans – Richards and, later, his protégé Richie Richardson – and Antiguan players like fast bowler Curtly Ambrose and wicket-keeper Ridley Jacobs have continued to feature prominently in the side. Small wonder, perhaps, that at times people appear to talk of little else.

▲ VIV RICHARDS' CRICKET BAT

St John's Cathedral

Newgate Street, west of Church Lane. Daily 9am–5pm. Free. The imposing twin towers of the Cathedral Church of St John the Divine are the capital's dominant landmark. A simple wooden church was first built on this hilltop site in 1681 and, after heavy destruction was wrought by a number of earthquakes and hurricanes, the present cathedral was put up in 1847.

From the outside, the grey-stone Baroque building is not particularly prepossessing – it's squat and bulky, and the two towers are capped by slightly awkward cupolas. More attractively, the airy interior of the cathedral is almost entirely encased in dark pine, designed to hold the building together in

▲ ST JOHN'S CATHEDRAL

nationhood. There are not necessarily any reminders of this past – just a collection of drab office buildings and residences and a constant flow of traffic – but you'll almost certainly find yourself on this road at some point, en route to somewhere more interesting. Still, the story itself is compelling.

By the time of World War II, life for the vast majority of Antiguans was very tough. There was widespread poverty and unemployment across the island, while for those who did have work on the plantations, hours were long and conditions onerous. In 1938, the Moyne Commission was sent from London to report on social conditions in the West Indies, and recorded that Antigua was among the most impoverished and neglected islands in the region. The commission recommended reform to the island's stringent laws banning trade unions, and in the following year the Antigua Trades and Labour Union (ATLU) was formed.

the event of earthquake or hurricane. The walls are dotted with marble tablets commemorating distinguished figures from the island's history, some of them rescued from the wreck of earlier churches on this site and incorporated into the new cathedral. In the grounds of the cathedral, the whitewashed and equally Baroque lead figures on the south gate – taken from a French ship near Martinique in the 1750s during the Seven Years' War between France and Britain – represent St John the Baptist and St John the Divine, draped in flowing robes.

Independence Avenue

Independence Avenue commemorates, at least in name, the long struggle for Antiguan

Within a few years the union had helped to improve conditions for plantation workers. Its major success came in 1951 when, under the leadership of former Salvation Army officer **Vere (V.C.) Bird**, workers refused to handle the sugar crop until their rates of pay were improved. For a year, the employers tried to starve the workers into submission, but they were eventually forced to concede a substantial pay rise. Subsequently, national confidence began to improve.

After the war, Antigua continued to be administered from afar by Britain's colonial office, but gradually the island's fledgling politicians were given authority for the day-to-day running of their country. The Antigua Labour Party, an offshoot of the ATLU, won the first local elections in 1946, and a decade later the island was given responsible ministerial government (meaning that the local people formed the government, though ultimate authority still lay with Britain). Ideological differences between the political parties – there were a variety of small parties, in addition to the larger ALP – were minimal, and all parties quickly came to support some form of independence from Britain. A constitutional conference was held in 1966, leading the following year to autonomy for the country in its internal and foreign affairs, although defence remained a matter for Britain.

Slowly, the national economy began to take strides forward, assisted (despite the closure of the last sugar plantations in 1971) by the development of tourism. By the elections of 1980 all parties considered that, politically and economically, the country was sufficiently mature for full independence and, following a further conference in Britain, the flag of an independent Antigua and Barbuda was finally raised on **November 1, 1981**. Since then, each year on this day an Independence Day Parade takes place at the Rec (see p.39).

The public market

At the south end of Market Street. Mon–Sat from around 6am until sunset. Home to the colourful public market, Market Street was once known as Scotch Row, in honour of the traders – many of them early Scottish immigrants who fled to the West Indies to escape the tyranny of seventeenth- and eighteenth-century English landowners – who once lined it

▼ BREADFRUIT

with shops selling sugar, indigo, coffee, tobacco and rum.

Today it remains an important shopping thoroughfare, the best place to head to for exotic fruit, vegetables and fish. As you'd expect, it's a lively, bustling place, particularly on Friday and Saturday, with a fine variety of food – for great snacking, head down and pick up some fresh, delicious sapodillas, papayas and mangoes.

The V.C. Bird statue

Right outside the public market is a large statue of V.C. Bird, who dominated Antiguan politics for half a century after taking over the leadership of the ATLU in 1943. Known as Papa Bird, he became the colony's first chief minister in 1956, its first premier in 1967 when

▼ THE V.C. BIRD STATUE

internal self-government was granted by Britain, and the first prime minister of an independent Antigua and Barbuda in 1981.

Though Bird has long been hugely popular with Antiguans, he and his entourage have also been consistently controversial. During his time in power, his government developed a reputation for doing business with all kinds of dodgy characters. There were allegations that ministers had brokered arms deals between Israel and the apartheid regime in South Africa, and even with the Medellin drugs cartel in Colombia. A British commission accused the government of "unbridled corruption", and the US – who kept a military base on the island and poured in over US$200 million in aid – of turning a blind eye, in an era when fear of radical governments (such as those of Cuba and Grenada) was the United States' leading concern.

Whatever the truth of the allegations, Vere Bird retained power until 1994 when, at the age of 84, he handed leadership of his party and the country to his giant son Lester, once Antigua's leading fast bowler and now probably its wealthiest man.

Accommodation

City View Hotel

Newgate Street ℡562 0256, ℻562 0242, ⊛www.carib-hotels.com /antigua/cityviewhotel. City centre hotel aimed at the business traveller, with 39 comfortable air-conditioned rooms, with cable TV, for US$94 single and US$118 double year-round. A good bet for cricket fans in town for a big game.

Heritage Hotel

Heritage Quay ☎462 2262, ℻462 1179, ✉heritagehotel@candw.ag. Right by the cruise-ship pier, this hotel is a decent option if you're in town on business; otherwise, it's completely missable. Spacious if rather drab rooms, all with their own well-equipped kitchens and priced from $100 year-round.

Joe Mike's Hotel

Corner of Nevis Street and Corn Alley ☎462 1142, ℻462 6056, ✉joemikes@candw.ag. Just a dozen rooms in this friendly place, right in the centre of town. Nothing special, but handy if you want to spend a night in the city. Rooms cost US$65 single or double. See overleaf for a review of *Joe Mike's* in-house eatery.

Silver Dollar Guest House

Corner of All Saints and Sheppard streets ☎464 3699. A short walk from the downtown market and bus station, this small, easy-going (though uninspiring) guesthouse has clean rooms with private baths and fans. One of the cheapest options on the island, charging US$40 for a double, or US$30 for a single.

Restaurants and bars

Big Banana – Pizzas in Paradise

Redcliffe Quay ☎480 6985 or 480 6986, ℻480 6989, ⊛www.bigbanana-antigua.com/pizzas.html. Mon–Sat 8.30am–midnight. Popular with tourists for lunch and dinner, *Big Banana – Pizzas in Paradise* has a pub-like atmosphere and serves food of reasonable quality – pizzas, salads and baked pota-toes, as well as more traditional Antiguan fish and chicken meals. Prices are decent, from EC$15 to EC$35, and you can eat either inside or outdoors under the trees.

Café Napoleon

Redcliffe Quay ☎562 1820. Mon–Sat 7.30am–5.30pm. At this French-owned café/bakery/patisserie, enjoy good breakfasts – freshly baked baguettes and croissants with butter, jam, pineapple juice and coffee for EC$14 – and, at lunchtime, excellent sandwiches (EC$15–25) on a shaded patio.

The Commissioner Grill

Between Redcliffe and Heritage quays ☎462 1883. Daily 10am–11pm. Excellent West Indian food is served all day in this popular and easy-going saloon, from tasty breakfasts of saltfish, eggs or fruit through to hearty suppers of fish, chicken and lobster (EC$25–75).

George

Corner of Market and Redcliffe streets ☎562 4866, ✉george@actol.net. Daily 8.30am–11pm. Right in the heart of the city, this lively restaurant serves top-notch West Indian food on a large, airy upstairs gallery decked out in sea-blues and -greens. The regular menu includes fire-roasted jerk shrimp and "chicken on a wire" (EC$35), while the weekend adds a number of Antiguan specialities including goat water, conch water, souse, rice pudding and pepperpot stew (EC$30–50).

Hemingway's

St Mary's St ☎462 2763, ⊛www.hemingwaysantigua.com. Mon–Sat 8.30am–11pm. Housed in an atmospheric, early nineteenth-century green-and-

(EC$26–34), elaborate main courses of fillet of snapper stuffed with shrimps in lobster sauce (EC$65), blackened jackfish in chilli garlic sauce (EC$55) or chicken breast with fresh mango and pineapple in a coconut curry sauce.

Joe Mike's

Corner of Nevis Street and Corn Alley ☎462 1142. Daily 7.30am–10pm. Unpretentious local eatery and small hotel (see overleaf) that's a popular lunchtime haunt for government ministers and other prominent Antiguans. Servings include large portions of ducana and saltfish, stewed pork, fungi and lingfish or barbecued ribs, all for around EC$15–25.

Mama Lolly's Vegetarian Café

Redcliffe Quay ☎562 1552. Daily 8.30am–4.30pm. Small, friendly café serving fresh-pressed juices and smoothies for EC$10–15. Also has a good vegetarian lunch menu, including lasagna, roti and red bean stew for no more than EC$23 for a large portion with salads.

O'Grady's Pub

Redcliffe Street ☎462 5392, @dennic@actol.net. Mon–Sat lunch & dinner. Popular place serving home-cooked English pub grub – shepherd's pie, steak and kidney pie, fish'n'chips and the like for EC$15–30 – on a veranda overlooking one of the city's main streets.

Papa Zouk

Hilda Davis Drive, Gambles ☎464 6044 or 464 7576. Mon–Sat 6pm–11pm. Imaginative Antiguan food served on a tiny patio festooned with flowers. The menu is small but interesting, with local produce thrown into dishes like Creole bouillabaisse

▲ CRAFT MARKET, REDCLIFFE QUAY

white wooden building, with a balcony overlooking the street and Heritage Quay, *Hermingway's* can be overwhelmingly crowded when the cruise ships are in; at other times, it's a great place to be, serving a range of excellent food, from sandwiches and burgers to fish and steak dinners (EC$25–50).

Home

Gambles Terrace, Lower Gambles ☎461 7651, ⑤461 0277, @www.thehomerestaurant.com, @home_c.r@candw.ag. Mon–Fri dinner only, Sat lunch & dinner. Closed June & July. Attractive restaurant in a converted home, a little ways from the centre of town, serving "Caribbean haute cuisine". Look for tasty starters of fish cakes or lobster cakes or a seafood medley (EC$35–55).

Philton's Bakery Café

Gambles Medical Centre, Friar's Hill Rd ☏463 2253 or 462 9447. Mon–Sat 8am–8pm. On the outskirts of St John's, this café is a good option for breakfast or lunch, serving freshly baked breads, muffins and pastries as well as hot lunch specials like pasta, pizza and slow-roasted chicken (EC$10–25).

Shops

Bryson's supermarket

At the bottom of Long Street by the water. Mon–Sat 8am–9pm, Sun 9am–4pm. An enormous supermarket, with a fairly standard assortment of foodstuffs.

Long Street liquor stores

Long Street, between Market and Cross streets. These beautiful old liquor stores stock Antigua's Cavalier and English Harbour rums, as well as other, better Caribbean rums, including Barbados's Mount Gay Extra Old and Haiti's Barbancourt Reserve.

Woods Centre

Friar's Hill Road, 750m north from the junction of Cross and Newgate streets. Oozing local affluence, this American mall-style shopping centre is mainly targeted at Antiguan shoppers. Nevertheless, here you'll find Epicurean, the island's best-stocked (if fairly pricey) supermarket (daily 8am–10pm), as well as banks, fast-food outlets, a post office, a gym and plenty more. A courtesy bus runs to Woods Centre from the west bus station, near the public market.

Entertainment and nightlife

18 Karat

Church Street ☏562 1858. Thurs–Sun 10pm–late. Cover EC$10. Mainly frequented by young Antiguans, this clubbing hotspot plays a wide variety of Caribbean and international music. Has recently been attracting some tourists.

▼FABRIC SHOP

Deluxe Cinema

High Street ☎462 2188. Ticket price EC$10. The island's only cinema, showing the latest imports from the US.

Traffic

Corner of Indpendence Avenue and Redcliffe Street ☎562 2949. Nightly 8pm–late. Cover of EC$10 after 10pm. A popular new nightclub, which often features live jazz or blues.

The northwest coast

Just north of St John's, Fort Bay boasts a lovely stretch of sand and, at its southern end, the notable historical site of Fort James, one of the best-preserved colonial forts on the island. A little further north, Runaway Bay and adjoining Dickenson Bay constitute the island's main tourist strip, with a couple of excellent beaches and a host of good hotels and restaurants.

Fort Bay

Fort Bay is home to the capital city's most popular beach, a long, wide strand of grainy white sand that's packed with city-dwellers at weekends and holidays. At its northern end, you can hire beach chairs from *Millers*, which is also a good place to pick up a drink (see review, p.59). If you're in a souvenir-hunting mood, there's a vendors' mall nearby.

At the other end of the strip, 500 metres south, a host of food and drink stalls open up at busy times, transforming the place into a lively outdoor venue, with music blaring, fish frying and plenty of frolicking on the beach. If you want to swim, there's a protected, marked area at the top of the beach; elsewhere, though the water is normally fine, you'll need to watch out for occasional undercurrents.

Fort James

Together with Fort Barrington (see p.93) and St John's Fort on Rat Island, the eighteenth-century Fort James was designed to deter any ships from attacking the capital, which had been sacked by French raiders in 1666. Though earthworks were first raised here in the 1680s, the bulk of the fort wasn't put up until 1739, when the long enclosing wall was added. The place never actually fired a shot in anger, although its guns undoubtedly intimidated visiting vessels into paying the eighteen shillings levied to the fort's captain.

Today, though the fort is pretty dilapidated, it still offers plenty of atmosphere: unkempt, often windswept and providing

▼ CANNON AT FORT JAMES

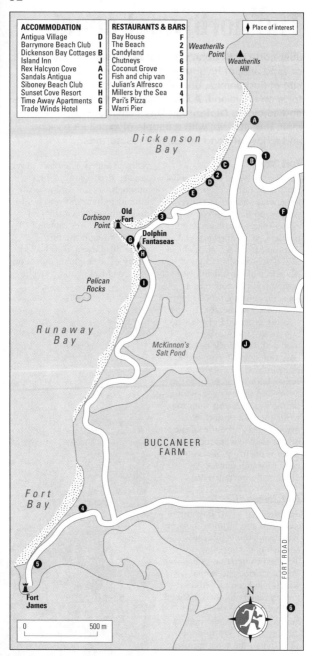

ACCOMMODATION

Antigua Village	D
Barrymore Beach Club	I
Dickenson Bay Cottages	B
Island Inn	J
Rex Halcyon Cove	A
Sandals Antigua	C
Siboney Beach Club	E
Sunset Cove Resort	H
Time Away Apartments	G
Trade Winds Hotel	F

RESTAURANTS & BARS

Bay House	F
The Beach	2
Candyland	5
Chutneys	6
Coconut Grove	E
Fish and chip van	3
Julian's Alfresco	I
Millers by the Sea	4
Pari's Pizza	1
Warri Pier	A

Place of interest

Weatherills Point

Weatherills Hill

Dickenson Bay

Corbison Point

Old Fort

Dolphin Fantaseas

Pelican Rocks

Runaway Bay

McKinnon's Salt Pond

BUCCANEER FARM

Fort Bay

Fort James

FORT ROAD

0   500 m

N

▲ RUNAWAY BAY

great views across the channel and back down to St John's harbour. Rusting British cannons from the early 1800s point out to sea and down the channel, their threat long gone but still a dramatic symbol of their era. Elsewhere, the old powder magazine is still intact, though leaning precariously, and the stone buildings on the fort's upper level – the oldest part of the structure, dating from 1705 – include the master gunner's house, the canteen and the barracks.

Runaway Bay

Most of the tourist development on Antigua has happened along the island's northwest coast, where quiet Runaway Bay (as well as the more built-up Dickenson Bay; see overleaf), offers gleaming white-sand beaches that slope gently down into the turquoise sea. Great for calm swimming, Runaway Bay has fewer hotels to tidy up their "patch", and so is strewn with more seaweed and rocks than Dickenson Bay. Still, it's a great place to wander in the gentle surf, though at the northern end much of the

beach has been eroded by heavy swells.

Dolphin Fantaseas

Runaway Bay ☎562 7946, ✉antigua@dolphinfantaseas.com, 🌐www.dolphinfantaseas.com. US$140 per half-hour session. At the northern end of Runaway Bay, Dolphin Fantaseas lets you swim with three dolphins in a man-made lagoon. It's not cheap, but it gets rave reviews from visitors. Others are less enthusiastic, some worried about the impact of captivity on dolphins, some complaining about "outsiders exploiting the island's resources". That said, the operation is certainly trying to address animal welfare concerns with an active local education programme on marine life and conservation. The business is also building up quite a menagerie of other attractions, including a mini-zoo with parrots, a toucan, tortoises, stingrays and hermit crabs.

Corbison Point

Just beyond the dolphins, grassy Corbison Point pokes out into the sea, dividing Runaway Bay from Dickenson Bay. A stone

▲ CORBISON POINT

igloo-shaped powder store is the sole remnant of an eighteenth-century British fort that once stood here. The cliff has also revealed Amerindian potsherds and evidence that more ancient island-dwellers exploited flint in the area for their tools.

▼ DICKENSON BAY

Dickenson Bay

Trapped between two imposing sandstone bluffs, Dickenson Bay is fringed by a wide white-sand beach, which stretches for almost a mile between Corbison Point and the more thickly vegetated woodland of Weatherills Hill at its northern end. It's a lovely bay, shelving gently into the sea and with protected swimming zones dividing swimmers from the jet-skiers, windsurfers, waterskiers and parasailers who frolic offshore.

The northern half of the beach fronts some of the largest of Antigua's hotels, including the *Rex Halcyon Cove*, whose pier juts out into the sea and offers dining above the ocean, and *Sandals Antigua*, with its striking yellow pavilions (see p.56 for reviews of the hotels). As a result, particularly in high season, the area can get pretty busy, with a string of bars, hair-braiders and T-shirt sellers doing a brisk trade. Still, it remains an easy-going place, with minimal hassle.

PLACES The northwest coast

In addition to the salt pond, seabirds can also be seen at either end of Dickenson Bay and at the north end of Runaway Bay, swooping gracefully around the sandstone bluffs; watch out in particular for the pelicans, showing off their clumsy but spectacular technique of divebombing for fish. See also Fitches Creek Bay, p.63, and Barbuda, p.102.

McKinnon's Salt Pond

A good place for bird-spotting, McKinnon's Salt Pond is an extensive area of brackish water edged by mangroves. More than 25 species of water birds have been recorded here, most noticeably the big flocks of sandpipers wheeling above the pond, as well as terns and plovers that nest on the sand and redfooted herons that breed in the mangroves.

Accommodation

Antigua Village

Dickenson Bay ☎462 2930, ⑤462 0375, ⑩www.antiguavillage.net. Large if unremarkable resort with dozens of self-catering apartments – from studios to two-bedroom flats, starting at around US$270/160 in winter/summer – strewn about attractively landscaped gardens. It's set on a good stretch of beach, there's a small swimming pool and a grocery store on site, and it's close to one of the area's best restaurants, *The Beach* (see review, p.57).

Barrymore Beach Club

Runaway Bay ☎462 4101, ⑤462 4140, ⑥barrymore@candw.ag. A reasonably priced option (US$115/75 in winter/summer) on a small piece of land with its own tiny, virtually private beach. There's a quiet, secluded feel to the place, and the rooms,

studios and one-bedroom apartments, are comfortable if unspectacular – ask for one close to the sea. The gardens are well kept and dotted with hibiscus and all types of palm. *Julian's Alfresco*, one of the best restaurants on the island, has recently opened on the premises (see review, p.58).

Dickenson Bay Cottages

Dickenson Bay ☎462 4940, ⑤462 4941, ⑩www.dickensonbaycottages .com. Thirteen spacious, airy and attractively furnished cottages set around a well-landscaped garden and medium-sized pool, up on a hillside overlooking Dickenson Bay. Though a quiet place, it's just a short walk from the beach and from the much busier *Rex Halcyon Cove* (see overleaf), where guests enjoy subsidized use of the facilities, including tennis courts and sun-loungers. One-bedroom cottages cost US$145/127 for two people in winter/summer (US$46 per additional person, though kids under 12 stay free), while two-bedroom cottages cost US$277/226 for up to four.

Island Inn

Anchorage Road ☎462 4065, ⑤462 4066, ⑩www.antigua-vip.com A kilometre or so north of St John's, this small two-storey hotel is curiously located another kilometre from the beach (on Runaway Bay) and targets mostly business travellers. That said, it's a cosy place with a small pool and good value at US$80/75 for a double room in winter/summer.

Rex Halcyon Cove

Dickenson Bay ☎462 0256, ℱ462 0271, ⓦwww.rexcaribbean.com. Very large, sprawling low-rise resort at the northern end of the beach, rather faded and a little time-worn but with good-sized rooms, a decent pool, tennis courts and a restaurant on the Warri pier – called, fittingly, *Warri Pier* (see review p.59). Rooms start at US$280/230 in winter/summer.

Sandals Antigua

Dickenson Bay, ☎462 0267, ℱ462 4135, ⓦwww.sandals.com. Part of the popular, all-inclusive chain found throughout the Caribbean, this resort has 189 luxury rooms that are cleverly spread throughout the resort, reducing the sense of being part of a crowd. Four restaurants offer excellent Italian, Japanese, southern US and international

food, and all watersports – including diving (training, certification and dives) – are included in the daily rate. Priced from around US$225 per person per day, though (heterosexual) couples only are allowed.

Siboney Beach Club

Dickenson Bay ☎462 0806, ℱ462 3356, ⓦwww.siboneybeachclub.com. Small, intimate and very friendly place, fabulously landscaped in a micro-jungle of its own. Rooms are spacious and comfortable, and one of the island's best restaurants (*Coconut Grove*; see p.58) is on site. Owner Tony Johnson is a great host and, now in his seventies, still windsurfs daily just offshore. A suite – which includes bedroom, lounge, kitchenette and patio or balcony – costs from US$170/110 in winter/summer. The choicest ones are right up in the jungle "canopy" with great ocean views.

Sunset Cove Resort

Runaway Bay ☎462 3762, ℱ462 2684. Situated at the northern end of the bay, *Sunset Cove*

▼ MCKINNON'S SALT POND

Resort has lost its beach entirely in heavy sea swells, and you have to walk five minutes around the headland to swim comfortably. That problem aside, it's a pleasant place, attractively landscaped with birds nesting in the bougainvillea. There's a small freshwater pool, and the sizeable rooms (from US$100 year-round) all come with kitchen facilities and cable TV.

Time Away Apartments

Runaway Bay ☎462 0775. Right next to *Sunset Cove* (see above) and suffering from the same beach erosion, this little block offers six one-bedroom apartments with tiled floors, rattan furniture (including pull-out couches, so that the rooms can sleep four at a pinch) and self-catering facilities. Apartment prices are US$125/100 a night year-round.

Trade Winds Hotel

Dickenson Bay ☎462 1223, ℱ462 5007, ⓦwww.antiguatradewindshotel .com. Lovely place in the hills above the bay, with big, comfortable air-conditioned rooms. Guests can chill out by the lagoon pool on a wide verandah overlooking the ocean or take the regular shuttle down to the beach, a kilometre away, where sun-loungers are freely available. The hotel's *Bay House* restaurant (see review, below) has good-quality food and great views. Double rooms start at US$225/125 in winter/summer.

Restaurants and bars

Bay House

At the *Trade Winds Hotel*, Dickenson Bay ☎462 1223. Daily 7am–11pm.

This smart restaurant, on an airy terrace high on the hill overlooking Dickenson Bay, is an ideal romantic place for a sunset drink followed by top-flight food. Creative, tasty starters set the tone – pork and prawn wontons (EC$25) or snapper ceviche (EC$30), for example – while main courses might include tuna with breadfruit and pineapple salsa (EC$65), grilled lobster with lime and garlic sauce (EC$75) or fillet of beef marinated in soy sauce with Chinese cabbage (EC$70).

The Beach

Dickenson Bay ☎480 6940, ℱ480 6943, ℮thebeach@candw.ag, ⓦwww.bigbanana-antigua.com/beach.html. Daily 8.30am–midnight. Newly refurbished and brightly painted restaurant on the beach right by the *Antigua Village* (see review, p.55), serving good food all day. Lunches see sushi, pizzas, burgers and salads served for EC$35–50, while dinner specials could include sesame-crusted tuna, meaty pasta or seafood stew for EC$40–75. Often has live music in the evenings (see "Nightlife", p.59).

Candyland

Fort James. Daily 9.30am–8pm. Friendly little beach bar under the casuarina trees just before you reach Fort James, serving good, simple food all day long. Regular specials include various curries, steamed fish and conch chowder, all for around EC$25–35.

Chutneys

Fort Road ☎462 2977. Tues–Sun dinner only. Five minutes' drive north of St John's, between *KFC* and *Pizza Hut*, *Chutneys* is the only authentic Indian restaurant on the island. They serve a wide variety of chicken, lamb and seafood curries (from mild to highly spicy; EC$39–45) as well as tandoori, tikka, rotis and some excellent vegetable dishes (EC$16). There's also a large non-curry menu that includes the bizarre-sounding but popular mako shark in champagne sauce (EC$45).

Coconut Grove

At the *Siboney Beach Club*, Dickenson Bay ℡462 1538, ℻462 2162, ℮coconut@candw.ag, ℗www.coconutgroveantigua.com. Daily 7.30am–11pm. Great cooking and friendly service combine at this delightful open-air beachside location. Mouthwatering starters include coconut shrimp in a coconut dip (EC$32.50), while main courses feature dishes like mahi mahi in a mango salsa (EC$62) and rock lobster in Creole sauce (EC$80). For dessert, try the magnificent coconut cream pie (EC$24).

Fish and chip van

Dickenson Bay ℡724 1166. Wed & Fri 4–9pm. If you're craving a round of fish (or sausage) and chips, look out for the fast-food van parked out on the main road between the *Marina Bay Hotel* and *Siboney Beach Club* most Wednesday and Friday evenings. A basket of fried fish and chips will run you EC$25, sausage and chips EC$15, and on Wednesdays, there's Indian curry at EC$25.

Julian's Alfresco

At the *Barrymore Beach Club*, Runaway Bay ℡562 1545 or 770 3233, ℮reservations@juliansantigua.com, ℗www.caribbeanhighlights.com/julian. Tues–Sun lunch and dinner. One of the top food choices on the island, with an appealing blend of Asian, European, South American and West Indian cooking styles and a lovely open-air location in tropical gardens just yards from the beach. Menu highlights include starters of seafood chowder for EC$16 and "fusion of fish" for

▼FISH AND CHIP VAN

▲ WARRI PIER

EC$34, while mains of Cajun-style mahi mahi and marinated tenderloin of beef cost EC$62 and EC$75, respectively.

Millers by the Sea

Fort James ⓣ462 9414. Daily 11am–11pm. Large beachside restaurant a kilometre or so north of St John's, with an extensive menu and occasional live music (see "Nightlife"). Typical dishes include curried conch or pan-fried snapper for EC$48, and there's normally a beach barbecue for lunch and dinner on Thursday.

Pari's Pizza

Dickenson Bay ⓣ462 1501. Tues–Sun 5.30–11.30pm. *Pari's Pizza* is all about pizzas, ribs and steaks – nothing earth-shattering, and slightly overpriced at EC$50 for a small rack of ribs, EC$24 for the smallest of the pizzas, and EC$69 for some surf and turf. Reasonable enough if you're staying nearby, though.

Warri Pier

At the *Rex Halcyon Cove*, Dickenson Bay ⓣ462 0256. Daily 11am–11pm. Open-air dining on what is now a rather shabby pier jutting out into the bay. American staples dominate the lunch menu, with burgers and BLTs for US$7–12, while the evening selection is more interesting, with fresh fish and steaks for US$15–25.

Nightlife

The Beach

Dickenson Bay ⓣ480 6940, ⓕ480 6943, ⓔthebeach@candw.ag, ⓦwww.bigbanana-antigua.com/beach.html. Regular live music on a stage set up just outside the restaurant on the edge of the beach. No cover charge unless there's a beach barbecue: "steak and stripe night" – a BBQ steak dinner with Red Stripe beer – costs EC$50.

Millers by the Sea

Fort James ⓣ462 9414. No cover charge. This large, convivial restaurant and bar sometimes hosts live music, ranging from local jazz and soca bands to guitarists and karaoke.

The Atlantic coast

Continuing east around the island from the top of Dickenson Bay brings you to Antigua's **Atlantic coast**. Here, the long jagged coastline, from Hodges Bay to Soldier Point at the southern end of Half Moon Bay, offers plenty of inlets, bays and swamps – but, with a couple of noteworthy exceptions, rather less impressive beaches.

Though tourist facilities on this side of the island are much less developed, there are still several places of interest. Betty's Hope is a partially restored sugar plantation; Parham, the island's first port, has a lovely old church; Devil's Bridge offers one of the most dramatic landscapes on the island; at the delightful Harmony Hall you can relax with an excellent lunch and a boat ride to Green Island; and at picturesque Half Moon Bay you can scramble along a vertiginous clifftop path above the pounding Atlantic.

Hodges Bay

For the most part, Hodges Bay is a high-end residential area, though it does have one fine French restaurant in *Le Bistro* and an excellent family-oriented hotel in *Sunsail Club Colonna* (see pp.69 & 68, respectively, for reviews). If you want to make use of the latter's enormous swimming pool or top-quality sailing equipment – Hodges Bay is great for sailing, as strong winds typically blow across this north coast spot – day passes are generally available, at US$100 for a full day or US$55 for a half. There's also a good dive shop here called Ultramarine, offering the usual packages for certified or non-certified divers as well as "surface scuba" for children not yet old enough to subject their bodies to the rigours of diving to any depth; see p.119 for contact info. As for the beach itself, it's decent, but not particulary good for hanging out – rather, this part of the island is best for watersports fanatics (see also Jabberwock Beach, below).

Prickly Pear Island

Five minutes' boat ride from the beach at Hodges Bay. Prickly Pear Island is a small, uninhabited place with a nice beach and good snorkelling. On Tuesdays, Thursdays and Saturdays, a character called Miguel runs day trips out here from the beach at Hodges Bay for US$60, or US$30 for kids (☎460 9978 or 723 7814, ⓦwww.pricklypearisland.com). The price includes sunbeds, snorkeling gear and all-you-care-to-eat and -drink from a big buffet-style lunch of seafood and West Indian specialities.

Jabberwock Beach

An otherwise unremarkable spot, Jabberwock Beach has, because of its strong winds and relative seclusion, recently

▲ SAILING AT HODGES BAY

become the home of the
island's first kiteboarding
operation, KiteAntigua
(Ⓦwww.kiteantigua.com). This
new sport combines some of
the principles of windsurfing,
wakeboarding, power kiting and
just plain flying: a rider on a
board controls a huge, partly
inflated kite so that it pulls him
along the water and often
several feet into the air. Even if

it sounds too extreme a sport
(or indeed, too expensive – a
4hr beginner's course will set
you back a whopping US$200),
it's well worth stopping to
watch for a while.

Stanford Cricket Ground

Right by the airport, where
Texan banker and developer
Allen Stanford is presiding over
some major new developments,

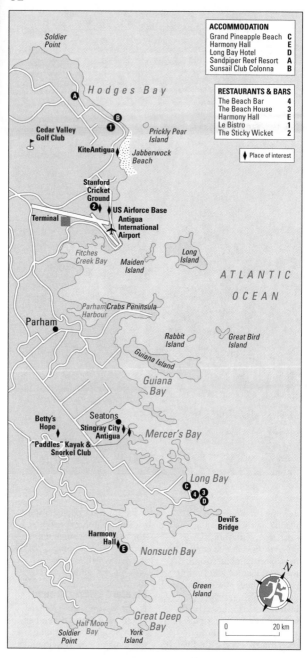

ACCOMMODATION

Grand Pineapple Beach	C
Harmony Hall	E
Long Bay Hotel	D
Sandpiper Reef Resort	A
Sunsail Club Colonna	B

RESTAURANTS & BARS

The Beach Bar	4
The Beach House	3
Harmony Hall	E
Le Bistro	1
The Sticky Wicket	2

♦ Place of interest

Soldier Point

Hodges Bay

A

B

1

Prickly Pear Island

Cedar Valley Golf Club

KiteAntigua ♦

Jabberwock Beach

Stanford Cricket Ground

2 ♦

US Airforce Base
Antigua International Airport

Terminal

Fitches Creek Bay

Maiden Island

Long Island

ATLANTIC

OCEAN

Parham Harbour

Crabs Peninsula

Parham

Rabbit Island

Great Bird Island

Guiana Island

Guiana Bay

Betty's Hope ♦

Seatons

Stingray City Antigua ♦

"Paddles" Kayak & Snorkel Club

Mercer's Bay

Long Bay

C

4 3

D

Devil's Bridge

Harmony Hall ♦

E

Nonsuch Bay

Green Island

Half Moon Bay

Soldier Point

York Island

Great Deep Bay

N

0   20 km

▲ CRICKET AT STANFORD CRICKET GROUND

including offices, shops, restaurants and a health club, you'll find the Stanford Cricket Ground, a spectacular new floodlit stadium with a pavilion, stand and restaurant, *The Sticky Wicket* (see review, p.69). The stadium doesn't host test matches (these will still be played at the Rec in St John's; see p.39) though it does serve as a practice pitch for international touring teams, as well as the venue for local games and day-night one-day matches.

Fitches Creek Bay

Fitches Creek Bay is a desolate inlet with no beaches of note, dotted with brackish mangrove swamps. It is, however, a great place for birdwatching: look out for herons, egrets and whistling ducks among the multitude of local species. For more good birdwatching sites, see the box on p.55.

St George's Parish Church

Overlooking Fitches Creek Bay, St George's Parish Church was first constructed in 1687 – though hurricane and earthquake damage have each long since taken their toll. Recent reconstruction of the place is largely complete, the church having been gutted and a new roof raised, but the ancient, weathered brick walls and crumbling tombs facing out to sea still lend it a strong sense of history.

St Peter's Parish Church

First settled in the seventeenth century, Parham, one of the oldest inhabited towns on the island, boasts the impressive, octagonal St Peter's Parish Church, considered unique in the Caribbean. A wooden church was first erected here in 1711, although the present structure mostly dates from 1840. The inside is spacious and airy, with tall windows capped

▲ BETTY'S HOPE WINDMILL

by brick arches, as well as a handful of marble tablets that commemorate nineteenth-century local notables. The unusual wooden ribbed ceiling is especially striking; the design – like an upturned ship's hull – has a delightful simplicity.

Parham Harbour

Outside St Peter's Parish Church, the cemetery tumbles down the hill towards Parham Harbour, Antigua's first port. Protected from the Atlantic waves by offshore islands, this fine natural anchorage was busy with oceangoing ships for more than two centuries until sugar exports slumped in the 1920s. Now it shelters yachts and small fishing vessels – there's a small jetty at the eastern end of town, but few other port facilities to testify to its heyday.

Betty's Hope

Tues–Sat 10am–4pm. Built in 1650, the partly restored Betty's Hope is Antigua's very first sugar estate. It was owned by the Codrington family for nearly two centuries, until the end of World War II. By that time, lack of profitability had brought the place to the edge of closure, which followed soon after.

Today, although most of Betty's Hope still lies in ruins, one of the windmills has been restored to working condition, and a small, interesting museum at the visitor centre tells the history of sugar on Antigua and explains the development and restoration of the estate.

St Stephen's Anglican Church

East along Collins Road, about 1.5km from Betty's Hope. The otherwise unremarkable St Stephen's Anglican Church has been rebuilt to a curious design, with the pulpit in the centre and the pews on each side. Meanwhile, outside the church, the crumbling tombs in the flower-strewn cemetery are testament to the fact that – in spite of the recent rebuild – the place has been a religious site for several centuries.

Seatons

The village of Seatons is the starting point for two very enjoyable, informative and well-organized **ecotour** attractions. The first, offered by Stingray City Antigua, allows you to swim with stingrays in their "natural" environment, a large penned area of ocean not far offshore (US$50 per person, US$35 for children; ☎562 7297, ⓦwww.stingraycityantigua.com). The second, offered by "Paddles" Kayak & Snorkel Club, is a half-day kayak tour of the nearby islands, inlets and mangroves, with an option to hike to sunken caves and snorkel in the North Sound Marine Park (US$50 per person, US$35 for children under 12; ☎463 1944, ⓦwww.antiguapaddles.com).

Devil's Bridge

1km east along track signposted off Collins Road. On a rocky outcrop edged by patches of grassy land, tall century plants and sunbathing cattle, Devil's Bridge takes its name from a narrow piece of rock whose underside has been washed away by thousands of years of relentless surf. The hot, windswept spot offers some of the most fetching views on the island, both back across a quiet cove and across the lashing ocean and dark reefs to a series of small islands just offshore.

En route back to the main road, a dirt track on your right after 400m leads down to a tiny but gorgeous bay – the perfect venue for a picnic. The place plays occasional host to some local parties, and can get rather litter-strewn, but the turquoise sea is exceptionally inviting and the usually empty strip of white beach a great place to chill out.

Long Bay

Though Long Bay is home to a couple of rather exclusive all-inclusives, the *Long Bay Hotel* and *Pineapple Beach* (see p.67), this doesn't stop you from getting access to a great, wide bay, enormously popular with local schoolkids, who can often be found splashing around or playing cricket at one end of the beach. The lengthy spread of white sand is protected by an extensive reef a few hundred

▼DEVIL'S BRIDGE

metres offshore, so be sure to bring your snorkelling gear. There's also a great little beach bar and a more upmarket restaurant (*The Beach House*; see p.68), good for shelter and refreshment when you've had enough sun.

Harmony Hall

The restored plantation house at Harmony Hall is now home to a tiny, chic hotel (see opposite), one of the island's best restaurants (see p.68) and an art gallery that showcases exhibitions of local and Caribbean art from November through April. Though it's a ways away from the main tourist hangouts and a little awkward to reach (down some poor-quality roads), it's a relaxed, friendly and delightful place, well worth the detour.

Green Island

Five minutes' boat ride from the jetty at Harmony Hall. On deserted Green Island, the beaches are powdery and the snorkelling excellent. If you're not a guest at the *Harmony Hall* hotel (see opposite), there's a small charge

for the boat service – ask at the hotel bar.

Half Moon Bay

One of the prettiest spots on Antigua, Half Moon Bay boasts a kilometre-long semicircle of white-sand beach partially enclosing a deep-blue bay, where the Atlantic surf normally offers top-class bodysurfing opportunities. The isolation of this side of the island means that the beach is often pretty empty, especially since the 1995 closure, after Hurricane Luis, of the expensive hotel at its southern end.

Soldier Point

At the southern end of Half Moon Bay, the headland of Soldier Point marks the beginning of an excellent 45min circular hike. Where the beach ends you can clamber up onto the rocks and a trail – marked by splashes of blue paint along its entire length – that cuts left along the edge of the cliff. It's a moderately tough climb, with a bit of a scramble required in places, but worth the effort for some fine views out to sea and

▼HARMONY HALL ART GALLERY

▲ SAILING TO GREEN ISLAND

over the bay and – apart from butterflies and seabirds – a sense of splendid isolation. Don't go barefoot, though: the rocks are sharp in places and there are plenty of thorns around.

Accommodation

Grand Pineapple Beach

Long Bay ☎463 2006, ⨍463 2452, ⓦwww.allegroantigua.com. Sprawling but attractively landscaped all-inclusive, with 130 rooms (US$500/400 in winter/summer) scattered alongside a lovely stretch of beach. The place can feel crowded, but the facilities – including four tennis courts and free non-motorized watersports – are good and there are plenty of activities laid on to distract you. Three restaurants mean you get a bit of variation for your evening meal, and there's a piano bar.

Harmony Hall

Brown's Bay Mill ☎460 4120, ⨍460 4406, ⓔharmony@candw.ag, ⓦwww.harmonyhall.com. A small, delightful Italian-run place in the middle of nowhere, open

from November to mid-May only. There are six simple but stylish rooms, which go for US$165, with tiled floors, large bathrooms, comfortable beds and small patios. The beach isn't up to much, but a small free boat regularly ferries guests out to the clean white sand at Green Island, five minutes away (see opposite). The restaurant (see overleaf) is classy and normally busy; when it's closed (as it is at dinnertime during the week), the hotel lays on separate food for guests. Don't come here for anything other than total peace and quiet.

Long Bay Hotel

Long Bay ☎463 2005, ⨍463 2439, ⓦwww.longbayhotel.com. Closed Sept & Oct. A small all-inclusive located in a fabulous setting by a tiny turquoise bay, with twenty cosy rooms, five cottages and a real feeling of isolation. Don't expect anything flash – the hotel owner and his friendly staff pride themselves on keeping everything very low-key and relaxed. That said, there are a few sailboats and windsurfers, a good tennis court, a big library and a games room with table tennis and board games. The chef is excellent and the bartender makes the best rum punch on the island. Rooms start at US$345/236 in high/low season for two, including breakfast and dinner.

Sandpiper Reef Resort

Boons Bay ℡462 0939, ℻462 1743, ⓦwww.sandpiper-reef.com. Tucked away on the north coast, this reasonably priced option (US$100/88 in winter/summer) has seen better days, though the beach is nice and quiet and you're only a short drive away from some of the best windsurfing locations on the island, as well as kiteboarding at Jabberwock Beach (see p.60). On the downside, you'll need a car to get anywhere beyond the hotel.

Sunsail Club Colonna

Hodges Bay ℡462 6263, ℻462 6430, ⓦwww.sunsail.com. Attractive north coast resort, Mediterranean in design – red-tiled roofs and pastel shades throughout – well landscaped and with the most spectacular pool on the island. The beach is pretty ordinary, but the solitude is addictive (though the hotel itself can get quite crowded). Most guests are staying on an all-inclusive package, many taking part in the windsurfing and sailing schools and many with young ones – this is one of the most child-friendly hotels on the island, with kids' clubs for all ages. There's also a good dive shop and a "body zone" for manicures, massages, etc. Readers of a leading British Sunday newspaper rated the place best-value resort in the world – rooms go from US$200/150 in winter/summer.

Restaurants and bars

The Beach Bar

Long Bay. Daily for lunch only. Often lively local spot right on the beach that makes for a great place to take a break from the sun and surf. Chicken and rice, burgers or fish and chips for EC$15–25.

The Beach House

At the *Long Bay Hotel*, Long Bay ℡463 2005. Daily for lunch only. Good selection of salads, sandwiches and fish (EC$25–40) at this casual terrace restaurant next to a beautiful stretch of beach. When cruise ships are in at St John's, it can get crowded for a couple of hours in the middle of the day, as many passengers are told that Long Bay has the best beach on the island, and that they should take a taxi ride over for a brief visit.

Harmony Hall

Brown's Bay Mill ℡460 4120, ℻460 4406, ℮harmony@candw.ag, ⓦwww.harmonyhall.com. Daily 10am–6pm, Fri & Sat dinner also, closed May–Nov. Run by a charming Italian couple, this is one of the island's finer restaurants, even if it is set nowhere near anyplace else. Built around an old sugar mill, the elegant but simple food is served on a terrace overlooking the bay. The menu includes starters of pumpkin soup (EC$20), homemade mozzarella with beetroots (EC$26) and an extraordinary antipasto misto (EC$35); mains of lobster tortellini (EC$38) or red snapper in a light cherry tomato and white wine sauce (EC$65); and delicious desserts of crème brulée (EC$18) or deep-fried bananas in cinnamon (EC$20). Despite the long drive along a road that's seen better days, the place is always busy and well worth the trip.

Le Bistro

Hodges Bay ☎462 3881, ℻461 2996, ✉pgbistro@candw.ag, ⓦwww.lebistroantigua.com. Tues–Sun dinner only. Long-established and well-reputed restaurant with a calm vibe and good, unobtrusive service. The place lays on excellent, authentic French cuisine, including starters of onion soup for EC$22 and snails in garlic butter for EC$30, and mains of lobster fettucine (EC$70), stir-fried shrimps flambéed in brandy (EC$75) and duck in orange sauce (EC$75).

The Sticky Wicket

Pavillion Drive (next to the airport), Coolidge ☎481 7000, ℻481 7010, ⓦwww.thestickywicket.com. Daily for lunch and dinner. Brand new cricket-themed diner and sports bar right next to the Stanford Cricket Ground (see p.61). Even outside the cricket season, there's a good buzz here, with regular live music, TVs showing top sporting events, unusual cocktails and excellent food. Bar snacks like West Indian pork ribs and spicy jerk buffalo wings go for around EC$25, meat and fish mains cost no more than EC$50–65 and there's a nice kids' menu for EC$15. Even if you don't come here during your stay, it's the ideal place to wait for your plane home, as the airport's just a short walk away.

Falmouth and English Harbour

An essential stop on any visit to Antigua, the picturesque area around **Falmouth** and **English Harbour** on the island's south coast holds some of the most important and interesting historical remains in the Caribbean; it's now also the region's leading yachting centre. The chief attraction is the eighteenth-century Nelson's Dockyard, which was the key facility for the British navy that once ruled the waves in the area. Today it's a living museum where visiting yachts are still cleaned, supplied and chartered, with several ruined forts nearby, as well as an abundance of attractive colonial buildings on the waterfront, several now converted into hotels and restaurants.

Across the harbour from the dockyard, there is further evidence of Antigua's colonial past at Shirley Heights, where more ruined forts, gun batteries and an old

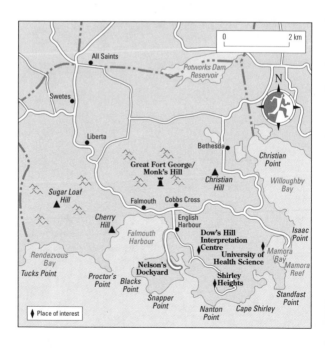

cemetery hold a commanding position over the water. It's a dramatic place whose rather forlorn air is shattered on Sunday evenings when steel and reggae bands lend sound to a lively (if somewhat over-touristed) barbecue party.

The area also has a handful of far less visited spots that repay a trip, including the massive military complex at Great Fort George, high in the hills above Falmouth, and the wonderful Rendezvous Bay – outstanding in an area with a paucity of good beaches; it's just a short boat ride or less than an hour's hike from Falmouth. Northwest of the area are the villages of Liberta and Swetes – the former notable as one of the first havens for freed slaves post-emancipation; the latter for its more recent connections with cricket.

Falmouth Harbour

This large, beautiful natural harbour has been used as a safe anchorage since the days of Antigua's earliest colonists, and the town that sprang up beside it was the first major settlement on the island. Today, though the harbour is still often busy with yachts, Falmouth itself is a quiet place, most of the activity in the area having moved east to English Harbour and Nelson's Dockyard (see p.74), divided from Falmouth Harbour by a small peninsula known as the Middle Ground (see p.77).

St Paul's Church

Right alongside Falmouth's main road. There's little in Falmouth to stop for, though you may want to pay a brief visit to St Paul's Church. The original wooden church (long since destroyed by

a hurricane) was the island's first, dating from the 1660s. Its modern brick successor is rarely open, but among the cracked eighteenth-century tombstones that cover the east side of the extensive graveyard is that of James Pitt, brother of the British prime minister, who died in English Harbour in 1780.

Rendezvous Bay

Although there is no beach of particular note in Falmouth, you can make a great hike from just west of town to Rendezvous Bay, the most idyllic and one of the quietest beaches on Antigua (see the box on p.73 for directions). Caressed by an aquamarine sea, and backed by coconut palms and dotted with driftwood, this curve of fine white sand is a gorgeous place to swim. The comparatively

Practicalities

A car is invaluable for touring around this area of the south coast. There are frequent buses between St John's and English Harbour, handy if you just want to explore Nelson's Dockyard, but to get up to Shirley Heights you'll certainly need your own transport or a taxi. See the listings on p.112 in Essentials for car rental, tours and taxi information.

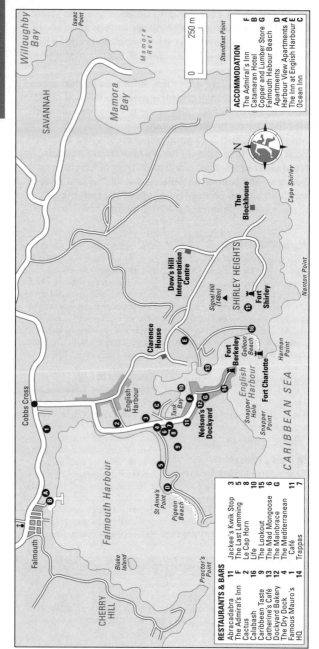

ACCOMMODATION
The Admiral's Inn   F
Catamaran Hotel   B
Copper and Lumber Store G
Falmouth Harbour Beach
Apartments   D
Harbour View Apartments A
The Inn at English Harbour E
Ocean Inn   C

RESTAURANTS & BARS
Abracadabra   11
The Admiral's Inn   F
Cactus   2
Calabash   16
Caribbean Taste   9
Catherine's Café   6
The Dry Dock   12
Famous Mauro's   1
HQ   14

Jackee's Kwik Stop   3
The Last Lemming   5
Le Cap Horn   8
Life   10
The Lookout   15
The Mad Mongoose   6
The Mainbrace   G
The Mediterranean
Café   11
Trappas   7

Getting to Rendezvous Bay

Heading out from Falmouth, turn left on Farrell Avenue and follow the road past the colourful Rainbow School onto a dirt track edged with banana groves. Take a right at the first intersection, past the Spring Hill Riding Club, then, at the fork, go left up a hill that soon becomes paved. There's a big, white house at the top of the hill; park near it and follow the track that veers off to the left. Driving a car, it should take around 5min to reach this point from the top of Farrell Avenue; on foot, it'll take about 25min.

The track climbs briefly between Cherry Hill and Sugar Loaf Hill, allowing great views back over Falmouth Harbour, then drops down through the scrubby bush, with sea grape and acacia trees on either side. After 25 to 40 minutes you'll reach a rocky bay strewn with conch shells; a further 10- to 15-minute wander along the beach brings you to Rendezvous Bay.

remote location means that there is rarely anyone else here, although the occasional boat trip makes its way across from Falmouth to use a thatched barbecue hut on the beach, which offers welcome shade. Bring some water, a picnic, a book and some snorkelling gear, and you could easily spend half a day here.

Great Fort George

High above Falmouth, and offering terrific panoramic views over the harbour and surrounding countryside, are the ruins of one of Antigua's oldest defences, Great Fort George (also known as Monk's Hill). The fort was constructed during the late seventeenth century, when England was at war with France. After the French navy captured the nearby island of St Kitts in 1686, the English decided to build Great Fort George on the hills behind the island's main town, together with housing and water cisterns to provide a secure retreat for Antigua's tiny population.

Though the French never in fact invaded, the fort was eventually completed in 1705, with dozens of cannons pointing in all directions;

barracks and gunpowder stores were added during the following century. By the mid-1800s, when any threat of invasion had receded, the fort was employed as a signal station, using flags to report on the movement of ships in and around Falmouth Harbour. Today, though much of the fort is in a very ruinous state, it's still well worth the effort to get to for the fabulous views and – as there's rarely anyone here – a quiet but evocative sense of the island's past. Upon arrival, you'll notice that much of the enormous stone perimeter wall remains intact. Meanwhile, inside the main gate and to the right, the west gunpowder magazine (built in 1731) has been well restored. It's fun to wander around the rest of the extensive scrub-covered ruins and see if you can identify which part was living quarters and which part military establishment.

To reach the fort, you'll either need to be driving a 4WD vehicle or take a thirty-minute hike: a precipitous but passable track leads up from the village of Cobbs Cross, east of Falmouth. Alternatively, from Liberta (north of Falmouth; see

▲ ENGLISH HARBOUR

p.81), take the inland road to Table Hill Gordon, from where another track winds up to the fort.

English Harbour

The road east from Falmouth leads to the tiny village of Cobbs Cross, where a right turn takes you down to the small village of English Harbour, which today consists of little more than a handful of homes, shops and restaurants. Nelson's Dockyard (see below) is the real attraction here.

Nelson's Dockyard

Daily 8am–6pm. US$5 or EC$13. Entry fee also covers Shirley Heights (see p.78). Adjacent to a fine natural harbour, one of Antigua's definite highlights is the eighteenth-century Nelson's Dockyard, the only surviving Georgian dockyard in the world. Though construction began in 1743, most of the present buildings date from between 1785 and 1792. Many of these buildings – such as the atmospheric *Admiral's Inn* hotel; see p.82 for review – were built from the ballast of bricks and

stones brought to the island by British trading ships, who sailed "empty" from home en route to loading up with sugar and rum.

The place developed primarily as a careening station, where British ships were brought to have the barnacles scraped from their bottoms and generally be put back into shape. The dockyard provided a crucial function for the military, providing them with a local base to repair, water and supply the navy that patrolled the West Indies and protected Britain's prized colonies against enemy incursion. However, during the nineteenth century, the advent of steam-powered ships, which needed less attention, coincided with a decline in British interest in the region, and the dockyard fell into disuse, finally closing in 1889.

Over the next sixty years the various dockyard buildings took a battering from hurricanes and earthquakes, until the 1950s saw a major restoration project; in 1961 the dockyard was officially reopened as both a working harbour and a tourist attraction. It was only then that the area got the name "Nelson's Dockyard" – apparently, the Antigua tourist board decided that a famous title was needed to market the place, and so they named it after the heralded British admiral, who as a young man was posted here for three years. Ironically enough, Nelson didn't like the island at all: he referred to Antigua in his correspondence as "a vile spot" and "this infernal hole".

Nevertheless, today the dockyard is a delightful place to wander around. To get here, follow the main road south from English Harbour, which ends at a parking area. From there, the entrance to the dockyard takes you past the local post office, a bank and a small covered market, where vendors compete languidly for custom on their T-shirts and other local souvenirs.

▲ THE ADMIRAL'S INN

The Admiral's Inn

Nelson's Dockyard. Beyond the dockyard's mini-commercial zone, the first building on your left is *The Admiral's Inn*, built in 1788 and originally used as a store for pitch, lead and turpentine, with offices for the dockyard's engineers upstairs. Today the place operates as a hotel and restaurant (see reviews, pp.82 & 83), yet the conversion has taken care to retain the original feel of the place, leaving an appealing atmosphere redolent of the dockyard's long history. Adjoining the hotel, a dozen thick, capped stone pillars –

looking like the relics of an ancient Greek temple – are all that remain of a large boathouse, where ships used to be pulled in along a narrow channel to have their sails repaired in the sail-loft on the upper floor.

The dockyard museum

Nelson's Dockyard. Daily 8am–6pm. Free. Down a lane from *The Admiral's Inn*, just beyond various restored colonial buildings and a 200-year-old sandbox tree, you'll come to the Admiral's House, a local residence (never actually used by an admiral) which was built in 1855 and today serves as the dockyard's museum.

The museum is worth a quick tour for its small but diverse collection that focuses on the dockyard's history and on Antigua's shipping tradition,

▲ DOCKYARD MUSEUM

with models and photographs of old schooners and battleships. Also look out for the cups and records celebrating the various races held during the annual Sailing Week, when English Harbour almost disappears under a tide of visiting yachts, their owners and crews (see box, below). Finally, right across the street from the museum is Terrence Sprague's **Heavenly Hill Art Gallery**, a great place to see colorful local artwork.".

Officers' quarters at Nelson's Dockyard

Just beyond the bougainvillea-festooned *Copper and Lumber Store*, which now serves as an elegant hotel and restaurant (see reviews, pp.82 & 86), are the officers' quarters – one of the most striking buildings in the dockyard, with a graceful double staircase sweeping up to a long, arcaded verandah. Ships' officers lived here during the hurricane season, when most of the fleet put into English Harbour for protection. The building sits on a huge water cistern of twelve separate tanks, with a capacity for 240,000 gallons of water, and today provides space for an art gallery, boutique, bar and other stores. The downstairs offices house the immigration and customs authorities.

Fort Berkeley

The narrow path that leads from behind the *Copper and Lumber Store* to Fort Berkeley is easily overlooked, but a stroll around these dramatic military ruins should be an integral part of

(see reviews, pp.82 & 86)

Sailing Week

Begun in 1967 with a tiny fleet of wooden fishing boats, and now regularly graced by over 200 quality yachts, the English Harbour Race is the centrepiece of Antigua's **Sailing Week**, a festival of racing and partying that transforms the area around Nelson's Dockyard into a colourful, crowded carnival village and the harbour into a parking area for every type of sailing boat. Don't expect to find a lot of Antiguans present – it's predominantly a party for the American and European sailing contingent – but if you're on the island in late April/early May it's a good place to see some superb sailing action and squeeze in a heavy night of bar-hopping.

▲ FORT BERKELEY, ENGLISH HARBOUR

your visit to the area. Built onto a narrow spit of land that commands the entrance to English Harbour, the fort was the harbour's earliest defensive point and retains essentially the same shape today that it had in 1745.

The path leads down to the water's edge; go around the jetty and some steps take you up to a trail leading to the fort, ten minutes' walk away out onto the headland. On your right as you approach, above the craggy wave-swept rocks, cannons once lined most of the wall facing out to sea, with the main body of the fort at the far end of the walkway comprising sentry boxes, a recently restored guardhouse and a gunpowder magazine or store. A handful of early nineteenth-century Scottish cannons are still dotted around the ruined fort, and the place offers spectacular views out to sea and back across the sand-fringed harbour.

The Middle Ground

For some rather more strenuous hiking, a right turn just before you reach Fort Berkeley leads up a poorly defined track to the peninsula known as the Middle Ground, where more military ruins dot the landscape. It's a stiff clamber to the top of the hill, where a circular base is all that remains of the one-gun Keane battery that stood here until the early nineteenth century. Still, standing up here you'll get a clear picture of the strategic importance of the Middle Ground for defending both Falmouth Harbour to the west and English Harbour to the east.

Fort Cuyler

From the Middle Ground hill, a track leads down and then up to the remains of Fort Cuyler, where more gun emplacements and crumbling barracks walls stand as further testament to the military domination of the area. You'll need all your tracking skills to keep to the paths around here – goats and the occasional goatherd are the only users of the old soldiers' tracks these days, and there is a fair amount of prickly cactus and thorn bush to contend with – but the hike offers spectacular views over the harbours, the ocean and the desert-like landscape of the Middle Ground.

Pigeon Beach

Though there's not much in the way of beach around Nelson's Dockyard, a good place to head for some sand after sightseeing is Pigeon Beach, five minutes' drive or twenty minutes' walk west of the dockyard. As you head out, turn left just before the harbour and follow the road past a series of restaurants and the Antigua yacht club. Keep going past the *Falmouth Harbour Beach Apartments* (see p.82 for a review), take the uphill track that goes sharply left and follow the road down to the right, where you'll find a wide expanse of white sand. When the harbour is full of boats – for example, during Sailing Week or the Classic Yacht Regatta – the beach can get a little crowded, but generally it's a lovely, secluded spot. At time of writing, the excellent local beach shack, *Bumpkins*, was closed due to a fire, though plans are afoot to reopen soon.

Shirley Heights

Daily 9am–5pm. US$5 or EC$13. Entry fee also covers Nelson's Dockyard (see p.74). Spread over an extensive area of the hills to the east of English Harbour, numerous ruined military buildings offer further evidence of the strategic importance of this part of southern Antigua. Collectively known as Shirley Heights (although technically this is only the name for the area around Fort Shirley), it's an interesting area to explore, with a couple of hiking opportunities for the adventurous who want to escape the crowds completely.

The area is named after General Sir Thomas Shirley, who, as governor of the Leeward Islands, was based in Antigua from 1781 to 1791. At a time when British Caribbean possessions were fast falling to the French – Dominica in 1778, St Vincent and Grenada in 1779 – and with British forces in America surrendering in 1781, Shirley insisted on massive fortification of Antigua to protect the naval dockyard. Building continued

▼ RUINS AT SHIRLEY HEIGHTS

steadily for the next decade and, although the threat diminished after the French were finally defeated in 1815, the military complex was manned until 1854. Since then, it has been steadily eroded by a succession of hurricanes and earthquakes.

Clarence House

Shirley Heights. Following the road uphill from English Harbour, you'll pass the late eighteenth-century Clarence House, an attractive Georgian house built in 1787 for Prince William, Duke of Clarence (later King William IV), who was then serving in the Royal Navy. At the time of writing, the place is under renovation, and cannot be visited. However, upon completion, it will house a museum of the lives of people who have stayed here, including the duke, various governors-general of Antigua and the Leeward Islands, and the late Princess Margaret and the Earl of Snowdon, who spent their honeymoon here in 1960.

Galleon Beach

Shirley Heights. Past Clarence House, a right-hand turn-off leads down to *The Inn at English Harbour* (see review, p.83), as well as the attractive crescent of Galleon Beach, where numerous yachts are normally moored at anchor just offshore. With a huge, old anchor dragged up on shore, this is one of the best beaches on this part of the island; the calm, shallow waters are great for swimming (though not so suited for watersports).

Dow's Hill

Shirley Heights. If you ignore the turn-offs down to Galleon Beach and carry straight on you'll soon see the Dow's Hill Interpretation Centre, which, frankly, has virtually nothing to do with the history of the area and is pretty missable. Nevertheless, outside the centre you'll find the scant remains of the Dow's Hill Fort, while indoors there's a collection of local shells and a fifteen-minute "multimedia" exhibition, with an adult voice answering a

▼ GALLEON BEACH

child's questions about the country's history from the Stone Age to the present. Thrilling stuff, to be sure.

Cape Shirley and the Blockhouse

Shirley Heights. Beyond the Interpretation Centre, the road runs along the top of a ridge before dividing where a large cannon has been upended in the centre of the road. Fork left for the cliff called Cape Shirley, where you'll find a collection of ruined stone buildings – including barracks, officers' quarters and an arms storeroom – known collectively as the Blockhouse. On the eastern side a wide gun platform looks downhill to Indian Creek (see below) and beyond, to Standfast Point peninsula and Eric Clapton's enormous house, as well as out over the vast sweep of Willoughby Bay. Every year, stories leak out that Clapton and friends such as Elton John and Keith Richards have turned up to jam at one of the island's nightclubs – but don't count on seeing them.

Officers' quarters at Fort Shirley

Shirley Heights. If you take the right-hand fork at the half-buried cannon, the road will lead you up to the further ruins of Fort Shirley. On the right as you approach are the still grandly arcaded (though now roofless) officers' quarters, overgrown with grass and grazed by the ubiquitous goats.

The military cemetery

Shirley Heights. Opposite from the officers' quarters, across a bare patch of ground, are the ruins of the military hospital and, in a small valley just below the surgeon's quarters, the military cemetery. Here you'll find barely legible tombstones, dating mostly from the 1850s; disease – particularly yellow fever – was prevalent at that time. There's also an obelisk commemorating the men of the Dorset regiment, English soldiers who died while serving in the West Indies during the 1840s.

The Lookout

Shirley Heights. The road from English Harbour ends at Fort Shirley itself, where a restored guardhouse now serves as an excellent little bar and restaurant (see reviews, pp.85 & 87). Beyond the guardhouse, the courtyard of the Lookout – where once a battery of cannons pointed out across the sea – now sees a battery of cameras snapping up the fabulous views over English Harbour, particularly on Sundays when the tourists descend in droves for the reggae and steel bands.

Indian Creek

From the Blockhouse (see above) it's a short but steep downhill hike to the bluff that overlooks Indian Creek, where, scattered along the shoreline, some of the island's most important Amerindian finds have been made. The hike passes down through scrubby grassland tended by goats and strewn with cacti, including the rather phallic red and green Turk's head cacti. At the bottom of the hill there's a small, sheltered but rocky beach, not great for swimming. The path continues up through a wood of cracked acacia trees and onto the deserted bluff, which offers grand views over the creek and, further east, to Mamora and Willoughby bays.

▲ MAMORA BAY

Mamora and Willoughby bays

From Cobbs Cross, avoiding the right turn to English Harbour, the road runs east towards a couple of quiet bays, namely tiny Mamora and the huge curve of Willoughby. It's an attractive drive, though there is little specific to see; Mamora Bay is now dominated by the exclusive *St James Club*, while the road past Willoughby Bay winds up through pineapple fields towards the old Betty's Hope sugar plantation (see p.64) and the island's east coast. Unless you're staying at *St James*, Mamora Bay is pretty difficult to visit. Easier to reach is Willoughby Bay, though it's utterly deserted, with no hotels or beach bars, and exposed to the Atlantic; even on a calm day, the ocean is quite rough around here.

Liberta

Liberta was one of the first "free villages" established for emancipated slaves after Britain abolished slavery in 1807 and subsequently passed the Act of Emancipation in 1834. Today,

even though Liberta is one of the largest settlements on the island, you'll find little reason to stop off and explore. On the main road through town, though, take note of two very striking churches: one of these, the pretty, pink church of Our Lady of Perpetual Help, is just by the turn-off to Fig Tree Drive (see p.88), while the other is a little further south, an unusual-looking affair in local green limestone and red brick, with a red corrugated-iron roof and lovely stained-glass windows.

Swetes

Northwest of Liberta, Swetes is best known as the birthplace of cricketer Curtly Ambrose, the West Indies' leading fast bowler during the 1990s, and of present-day local cricketing hero Ridley Jacobs (see p.43 for more on the Antiguan passion for cricket). There's not much in the way of sightseeing here, apart from a surprisingly well-preserved sugar mill and a curious house built in the shape of a boat.

▲ THE COPPER AND LUMBER STORE

Accommodation

The Admiral's Inn

Nelson's Dockyard ☎460 1027, ℱ460 1153, ⓦwww.admiralsantigua.com. Built in 1788 as the dockyard's supply store and now attractively restored, this is one of the best accommodation options on Antigua, with great atmosphere, welcoming staff, a romantic setting by the harbour and sensible prices. The lovely old rooms, most with four-poster beds, run from US$130/90 in winter/summer. An occasional free boat ferries guests to a nearby beach.

Catamaran Hotel

Falmouth ☎460 1036, ℱ460 1339, ⓦwww.catamaran-antigua.com. Friendly little place on the north side of the harbour in Falmouth, adjacent to a small marina. The beach is not great for swimming, and it's a bit of a hike to the action at the dockyard, but the rooms are comfortable and good value, at US$105/85 in winter/summer.

The Copper and Lumber Store

Nelson's Dockyard ☎460 1058, ℱ460 1529, ⓦwww.copperlumberantigua .com. Very elegant Georgian hotel in the heart of the dockyard, used from the late eighteenth century as its name suggests, with a dozen superb rooms (US$325/275 in winter/summer), some fabulously furnished with mostly nautically themed antiques. Quiet at night, but a short walk from a handful of good restaurants.

Falmouth Harbour Beach Apartments

Falmouth ☎460 1094, ℱ460 1534. On the east side of the harbour, by a thin strip of beach, reasonably sized self-catering studio apartments with ceiling fans and ocean-front verandahs. The apartments are nothing spectacular but do offer decent value, at US$150/85 in winter/summer.

Harbour View Apartments

Falmouth ☎460 1762, ℱ463 6375, ⓦwww.antigua-apartments.com. Modern block with a small pool and six two-bed self-catering apartments, all overlooking the harbour, by a small and unexceptional beach. Good option for a family on a budget, as rooms sleep up to four and cost just $150/85 a night in winter/summer.

The Inn at English Harbour

English Harbour ☎460 1014, ℱ460 1603, ⓦwww.theinn.ag. Attractive old hotel, popular with repeat guests and spread over a large site beside the harbour, next to a pleasant white-sand beach. There are 22 elegant, comfortable rooms in a two-storey building bedecked in bougainvillea; prices start at US$300/155 in winter/summer.

Ocean Inn

English Harbour ☎463 7950, ℱ460 1263, ⓦwww.theoceaninn.com. Small, friendly inn perched on a hillside above English Harbour, with six doubles/twins and four cottages starting at US$95 a night in high season. It's some distance from a good beach, but there's a tiny pool and a nice opportunity to vary the pace between the spectacular views and relative peace and quiet of the hotel with what is often a party atmosphere in and around Nelson's Dockyard, just five minutes' walk down the hill.

Restaurants and bars

Abracadabra/ The Mediterranean Café

English Harbour ☎460 1732 or 460 2701, ℱ463 8084, ⓦwww.theabracadabra.com, ⒺWabra@candw.ag. Daily 10am–3pm and 7–11pm. Just outside the dockyard, *Abracadabra* offers a mostly Southern Italian menu of pastas, grilled meat and fish

(EC$30–50), with a cosy atmosphere and live music several nights a week. A little place called the *Mediterranean Café* sits next to the main restaurant, serving tasty and healthy shakes, smoothies and salads as well as baguettes and sandwiches (EC$10–20) from morning until mid-afternoon.

The Admiral's Inn

Nelson's Dockyard ☎460 1027. Daily 7am–9.30pm. Good, unpretentious dining in the old *Admiral's Inn* building or, more romantically, by the water's edge (take mosquito repellent), with occasional local dishes such as pepperpot stew among the more standard meals of fish, chicken and salads (EC$25–40).

Alberto's

Willoughby Bay ☎460 3007. Tues–Sun dinner only, closed July–Oct. Some of the best Italian food on the south coast, hosted by the eponymous longtime proprietor at an out-of-the-way spot. The evening's menu is chalked up on a blackboard; recurring entries include thin slices of breadfruit roasted in a garlic and parsley sauce (EC$25) and pan-fried tuna or wahoo with wasabi and ginger (EC$60). Top desserts, notably sorbets of coconut, lemon and passion fruit, send you happily on your way.

Cactus

Main Road, Falmouth Harbour ☎460 6575, ⓦwww.cactusclubantigua.com. Mon–Sat 4pm–late. Well-positioned restaurant on a big verandah with spectacular views over Falmouth Harbour and the Middle Ground. Inside, there's a lively bar area with two darts boards and three pool tables (tournaments every Monday and Thursday). Food is served in tapas-style portions with nachos at EC$15, fish dishes at EC$20 and grilled steak at EC$25.

Calabash

Galleon Beach ☎460 1452. Daily for lunch and dinner. Airy terrace restaurant close to the beautiful Galleon Beach (see p.79). Good salads at lunch for EC$20–25 and a world food tour for dinner with mains – including Jamaican jerk chicken, grilled Cajun-style mahi mahi, Calabash Indian curry, grilled steak, teriyaki salmon and Caribbean seafood stew – at up to EC$45.

Caribbean Taste

Behind Dockyard Drive, English Harbour ☎562 3049 or 460 1376. Daily for breakfast, lunch and dinner. Authentic Antiguan eats in this small restaurant tucked away among local residences just before the entrance to the dockyard. Servings include large portions of ducana and salt cod, fungi and conch stew, curried goat, jerk chicken and various kinds of rotis, all for around

EC$25–35. There are also some delicious and unusual local fruit juices including soursop, guava and passion fruit.

Catherine's Café

Antigua Slipway, English Harbour ☎460 5050. Wed–Mon for lunch and dinner, closed mid-May to mid-July. Across from Nelson's Dockyard, great food and wonderful views at this laid-back French café on a shaded terrace by the water's edge. The simple but imaginative menu includes clams, oysters, moules marinières and Sambuca prawns at EC$40–65 as well as some spectacular desserts, such as tarte tatin. You have to take a water taxi from the dockyard to get here or, if you've got a car, you can head in the direction of Shirley Heights and turn down the Antigua Slipway road.

Dockyard Bakery

Nelson's Dockyard ☎460 1474. Daily 8am–5pm. Nice place for breakfast or daytime snacks, selling guava danishes, pineapple turnovers and bread pudding (EC$5), all freshly baked in the dockyard's old kitchens.

▼CARIBBEAN TASTE RESTAURANT

The Dry Dock

Falmouth Harbour ☏460 3040. Daily for lunch and dinner. Good sports bar serving burgers, sandwiches and the like (EC$25–35). The joint regularly screens first-run movies, and there's a small club space called *Nitrox* in the back for late-night drinking and dancing (small cover charge).

Famous Mauro's

Cobbs Cross ☏460 1318. Daily for lunch and dinner. One of the best places for pizza on Antigua, with more than thirty types available daily (EC$15–25), all freshly cooked in the wood-burning oven.

HQ

Nelson's Dockyard ☏562 2563. Daily for lunch and dinner, bar open all day until late, closed Sun evenings. Excellent place in the heart of the dockyard, recently taken over by a French family and serving well-prepared seafood, steaks and chicken (EC$30–50). The long verandah at the back of the restaurant has lovely views down towards Fort Barrington, while inside a newly acquired antique French chandelier hangs over a cosy piano bar.

Jackee's Kwik Stop

Falmouth Harbour ☏460 1299. Daily for breakfast, lunch and dinner. One of the best of the local eateries run by the delightful Jackee, this little café sells traditional Antiguan food, with daily specials of ducana and saltfish, pepperpot stew and fungi or souse (EC$25–35).

The Last Lemming

Falmouth Harbour ☏460 6910, ℻460 6911, ✉lastlemming@candw.ag. Daily for lunch and dinner. Good food at this frequently crowded harbourside spot, though the service can be dreadfully slow. Pan-fried catch of the day and grilled steaks (EC$25–35) are typical of the daily offerings.

Le Cap Horn

Between Falmouth and English Harbour ☏460 1194, ℻460 1793. Fri–Wed 6.30pm–11pm, closed May–Oct. French-Peruvian chef Gustavo prepares specialities from different regions of France using local meats and fish (EC$35–60), while his wife Helene does the desserts in this mellow garden restaurant. There's also an excellent pizzeria with a wood-burning brick oven (pizzas EC$20–30).

Life

English Harbour ☏562 2353 or 723 3502, ✉lifebarantigua@yahoo.com. Wed–Mon for lunch and dinner, closed Sept. Decked out in primary colours, this lively bar and restaurant sits over the water on a pier just outside the dockyard. The dinner menu includes grilled fish and steaks, fish and chips, bangers and mash and various curries for EC$25–30; there's also a good kids menu for EC$15. Aphorisms on "life" are painted up everywhere and there's a chalkboard to add your own insights.

The Lookout

Shirley Heights ☏460 1785, ℻460 3490. Daily 9am–10pm. The only place for a refreshment break while you're up on the Heights, with a large patio providing superb views over the harbour and the dockyard. Simple meals such as roast chicken and burgers (EC$25–35) are the order of the day, with the Sunday (and, to a lesser extent, Thursday) barbecues pulling a huge crowd for the reggae and steel bands that play from early afternoon through to the late evening.

The Mad Mongoose

Falmouth Harbour ☎463-7900. Tues–Sun 10am–11pm. Just a stone's throw from the water, this often lively bar – which gets absolutely packed when the boats are in – serves snacks and simple meals like sandwiches and burgers (EC$15–25). Also has a games room and satellite TV.

The Mainbrace

At *The Copper and Lumber Store*, Nelson's Dockyard. Daily for breakfast, lunch and dinner. Good breakfasts for around US$8 at this Georgian inn; typical English pub lunches – burgers, chillies, etc – at around US$10; and in the evenings, more formal and more costly dining (entrées such as grilled steak and fish from US$25) in the *Copper and Lumber Store*'s stylishly renovated wardroom.

Trappas

Between Falmouth and English Harbour ☎562 3534. Daily (except Wed) from 6pm. A mixture of fairly standard English pub grub and tasty Thai food – shrimp in green curry sauce, mussels in ginger soup, Pad Thai noodles – at this popular bar: EC$20 for all starters, EC$30 for mains and EC$15 for desserts.

Entertainment and nightlife

Abracadabra

English Harbour ☎460 1732 or 460 2701, ✆463 8084. Nightly 7pm until late. No cover. Once dinner is over, the lights dim and *Abracadabra* (often) becomes a pretty hopping place: DJs spin R&B and 1980s dance music, while occasional live bands – jazz, reggae, rock – get patrons up for some open-air dancing

▼ STEEL BAND AT THE LOOKOUT RESTAURANT

on a small dance floor next to the restaurant (see p.83).

The Last Lemming

Falmouth Harbour ☎460 6910. Open nightly until late. No cover. Lively bar, particularly when the boats are in – it's right under the Antigua Yacht Club, with great views across the harbour. Often open later than anywhere else and featuring the occasional local band.

Life

English Harbour ☎562 2353 or 723 3502, ℮lifebarantigua@yahoo.com Daily except Tues, closed September. In the evenings, this bar and restaurant (see p.85) often becomes a vibrant party scene, playing Sixties and Seventies music in counterpoint to the more modern sounds coming from right across the street at *Abracadabra*. Popular with both the sailing crowd and the locals.

The Lookout

Shirley Heights ☎460 1785, ℗460 3490. Thurs 4–8pm & Sun 4–10pm. No cover. On Sunday and Thursday afternoons (Thursdays are less crowded), steel and reggae bands set up on the Heights overlooking English Harbour. There's a bar and barbecue, vendors selling trinkets and T-shirts and a great party atmosphere, though at the peak of the season you'll find little room to move.

The west coast

Tourism makes a firm impression on Antigua's **west coast**, with hotels dotted at regular intervals between the little fishing village of Old Road in the south and the capital, St John's, in the north. Two features dominate the area: a series of lovely beaches, with Darkwood probably the pick of the bunch for swimming, snorkelling and beachcombing, and, in the southwest, a glowering range of hills known as the Shekerley Mountains, offering the chance for a climb and some panoramic views.

On the edge of the Shekerly range, the lush and thickly wooded Fig Tree Hill is as scenic a spot as you'll find. A variety of good trails can be picked up in this area. Some lead inland, to sites usually overlooked by tourists such as Boggy Peak and Green Castle Hill, while one, the Rendezvous Trail, leads back east to Rendezvous Bay. Meanwhile, due west of St John's, the Five Islands peninsula holds several hotels, some good beaches and the substantial ruins of the eighteenth-century Fort Barrington.

Fig Tree Drive and Fig Tree Hill

The main road in the area, Fig Tree Drive, runs west from Swetes (see p.81) through the most densely forested part of the island, Fig Tree Hill. You won't actually see any fig trees – the road is lined with bananas (known locally as figs) and

▼ FIG TREE DRIVE

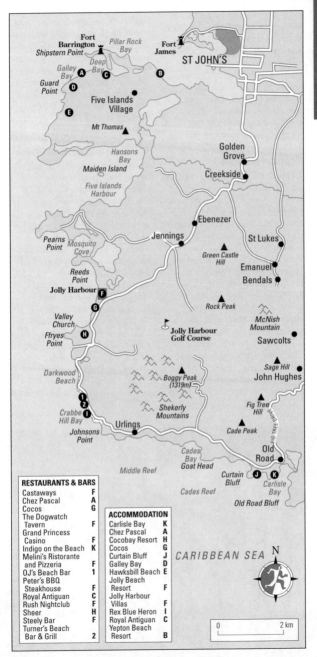

Fort Barrington
Shipstern Point
Pillar Rock Bay
Fort James
ST JOHN'S
Deep Bay
Galley Bay **A** **C**
Guard Point **B**
D
Five Islands Village
E
Mt Thomas

Golden Grove
Creekside

Hansons Bay
Maiden Island

Five Islands Harbour

Ebenezer
Jennings
St Lukes

Pearns Point
Mosquito Cove
Green Castle Hill
Emanuel
Bendals

Reeds Point
Jolly Harbour **F**
G
Rock Peak
McNish Mountain
Sawcolts

Valley Church
Ffryes Point **H**
Jolly Harbour Golf Course

Darkwood Beach
Sage Hill
John Hughes

1
2
Boggy Peak (1319m)
Shekerly Mountains
Fig Tree Hill

Crabbe Hill Bay **I**
Johnsons Point
Urlings
Cade Peak
Old Road

Cades Bay Goat Head
Middle Reef
Curtain Bluff **J** **K**
Carlisle Bay

Cades Reef
Old Road Bluff

CARIBBEAN SEA   **N**

RESTAURANTS & BARS	
Castaways	**F**
Chez Pascal	**A**
Cocos	**G**
The Dogwatch Tavern	**F**
Grand Princess Casino	**F**
Indigo on the Beach	**K**
Melini's Ristorante and Pizzeria	**F**
OJ's Beach Bar	**1**
Peter's BBQ Steakhouse	**F**
Royal Antiguan	**C**
Rush Nightclub	**F**
Sheer	**H**
Steely Bar	**F**
Turner's Beach Bar & Grill	**2**

ACCOMMODATION	
Carlisle Bay	**K**
Chez Pascal	**A**
Cocobay Resort	**H**
Cocos	**G**
Curtain Bluff	**J**
Galley Bay	**D**
Hawksbill Beach	**E**
Jolly Beach Resort	**F**
Jolly Harbour Villas	**F**
Rex Blue Heron	**I**
Royal Antiguan	**C**
Yepton Beach Resort	**B**

0   2 km

mango trees as it carves its way through mountains and tropical vegetation down to the south coast at Old Road (see below). About halfway along the drive, you can stop at a small roadside shack which calls itself the Cultural Centre, where you can get a drink and some fruit picked straight off the trees from local farms.

Rendezvous Trail

From the Cultural Centre shack on Fig Tree Hill, a track leads south to the Wallings Reservoir – the island's first – where you'll find picnic tables set up around the edge of the water. More serious hikers can take the Rendezvous Trail, which starts on your left just before you reach the steps of the reservoir. It crosses the Wallings Woodlands to the nearly always empty beach a two-hour walk away at Rendezvous Bay (see p.71).

Even a short stroll repays the effort: the woodlands are the best remaining example of the evergreen secondary forest that covered the island before British settlers arrived, with more than thirty species of shrubs and trees, including giant mahogany trees, and masses of noisy bird life. Bear in mind, though, that while it's pretty hard to get lost, the main path is little used and in places can quickly become overgrown and hard to make out.

Old Road and Carlisle Bay

Once an important port and town, Old Road derived its name from nearby Carlisle Bay – a safe anchorage or "road" for the early settlers – but was soon surpassed by the new "roads" of St John's and Falmouth Harbour. Today Old Road is a small and rather impoverished fishing village, though increasingly enlivened by the swanky *Curtain Bluff* resort – and a superb swath of beach – on the eponymous sandstone bluff, as well as the five-star *Carlisle Bay* hotel, which opened in late 2003 (see p.94 for reviews of both).

Many locals have recently become passionate supporters of

▼ SOUTHWEST ROAD, NEAR URLINGS

THIS BEACH IS KEPT CLEAN

BY

CHURCH OF GOD OF PROPHECY

SPONSORED BY ANJO GROUP OF COMPANIES

Please play your part...

▲ DARKWOOD BEACH

the English football club Liverpool and its star striker Emile Heskey; his father was born and lived in Old Road before moving to England in the 1960s.

Boggy Peak

Heading west from Old Road, the road follows the coast past a series of banana groves and pineapple plantations and around Cades Bay, offering delightful views out to sea over Cades Reef. On the right, a kilometre from Old Road, a track leads up into the Shekerley Mountains to Boggy Peak, which, at 400 metres, is the highest point on the island. The panoramic view from the top – in good visibility you can even make out St Kitts, Guadeloupe and Montserrat – is well worth the steep drive or one-hour climb. Unfortunately, the peak is now occupied by a communications station, safely tucked away behind a high-security fence, so you'll need to make arrangements to visit with Cable & Wireless in St John's (☎462 0840). If you haven't the time or the inclination, the views from outside the perimeter fence are almost as good.

Turner's, Darkwood and Coco beaches

Continuing west through the village of Urlings, the road runs alongside a number of excellent beaches. First up is Turner's Beach and Johnson's Point, where the sand shelves down to the sea beside a couple of good beach bars, including *Turner's* (see review, p.98), where you can also rent snorkelling gear.

The snorkelling is better just north of here at Darkwood Beach, a great spot to stop and take a swim, with a wide stretch of beach running right alongside the main road. Look out for small underwater canyons just offshore, and schools of squid and colourful reef fish. Beachcombers will find this one of the best places on the island to look for shells and driftwood. There are a couple of groves of casuarina trees for shade, as well as *OJ's*, another friendly little beach bar that offers inexpensive local food (see p.97).

Lastly, Coco Beach is reached via a turn-off signposted to the *Cocobay Resort* (see p.94); follow the track for 500 metres past some old sugar mills for another magnificent stretch of sand, again strewn with driftwood and edged by a turquoise sea.

Jolly Harbour

Day passes for *Jolly Beach Resort* US$50. Covering an immense area (much of it reclaimed swampland and salt ponds) north of Coco Beach, the 450-bedroom all-inclusive *Jolly Beach Resort* (see p.95 for accommodation review) sprawls alongside a mile of one of Antigua's best beaches, with clear blue water lapping against the sugary white sand. A day pass for the beach, available from the resort, includes lunch, drinks and use of the watersports equipment. Adjacent, the Jolly Harbour complex has a marina, rental apartments, a golf course, restaurants and a small shopping mall. It's a world apart from the "real" Antigua – like a small piece of America transplanted in the Caribbean.

Green Castle Hill

If you haven't climbed Boggy Peak (see overleaf) or Monk's Hill (aka, Great Fort George; see p.73), you could consider getting your panoramic view of Antigua from the top of Green Castle Hill. The peak is littered with natural formations of stone pillars and large rocks, which some believe are Stone Age megaliths left by Antigua's oldest inhabitants. The claim is patently absurd – there is no evidence of Antigua's Amerindians having either the technology or the inclination to erect such monuments to their deities – but don't let that put you off visiting. The views are superb,

▼KAYAKING AT FIVE ISLANDS

▲ HAWKSBILL ROCK

particularly to the north beyond St John's, and besides the odd goat, you won't see a soul around.

You'll really need a car to get here. Head inland from the main road between Jennings and St John's towards Emanuel; the path to the top (a forty-minute walk) begins by the gates of a small brick factory connected to a large stone quarry.

Five Islands peninsula

To the west of St John's the highway leads out through a narrow isthmus onto the large Five Islands peninsula, named after five small rocks that jut from the sea just offshore. There are several hotels on the peninsula's northern coast, a few more on its west coast, though the interior is largely barren and scrubby, and there's not a huge amount to see.

Hawksbill Bay

To reach Hawksbill Bay and some more excellent beaches,

follow the main road straight through Five Islands peninsula, ignoring the turn-offs for the *Yepton Beach Resort* and *Chez Pascal* (see pp.96 & 94, respectively). A kilometre offshore from the bay, a large rock in the shape of the head of a hawksbill turtle gives the place its name.

Fort Barrington and Deep Bay

On Goat Hill, at the northern point of Five Islands peninsula. Close to the *Royal Antiguan* hotel (see p.96), the circular stone ruins of Fort Barrington overlook the gorgeous Deep Bay. The British first built a simple fort here in the 1650s, to protect the southern entrance to St John's Harbour, though it was captured by the French when they took the city in 1666. In 1779, at a time of renewed tension between the two nations, Admiral Barrington of the British navy enlarged and strengthened the fort. This time, the deterrent proved effective; like most of Antigua's defences, Fort Barrington never saw any further action, and spent the next two centuries as a signal station reporting on the movement of ships in the local waters.

Today, it's well worth the 20min walk around the beach at Deep Bay and up the hill to the fort. Once arrived, you'll be treated to a dramatic sense of isolation as you look out to sea or back over the tourists sunning themselves far below on the bay.

Accommodation

Carlisle Bay

Old Road ☎484 0000, ℻484 0001, ⓦwww.carlisle-bay.com "Barefoot luxury" – ie, luxury in a beach setting – is the overriding theme at this brand-new resort. At a starting price of US$595 a night for a room with breakfast and afternoon tea, it's clearly not for everyone. But, it's beautifully designed – in low-key whites and greys with polished dark-wood furniture – and set in the most fabulous location, the 88 suites facing a peaceful white-sand beach with the dense forests of Fig Tree Drive all around. There's a gym, a spa, a 45-seat cinema, a thoughtfully constructed library, two excellent restaurants (*Indigo on the Beach* and *East*) and, for those who can't leave their work behind, easy access to the Internet.

Chez Pascal

Galley Bay Hill, Five Islands ☎727 8384, ⓦwww.chezpascal.net. In addition to being a French restaurant (see p.96), *Chez Pascal*, set in tropical gardens on a hillside above Galley Bay, also has four luxurious guestrooms. Come here for fine French food, great views and bed-and-breakfast at US$175/150 in high/low season.

Cocobay Resort

Ffryes Beach ☎562 2400, ℻562 2424, ⓦwww.cocobayresort.com. Excellent all-inclusive right by the beach, with twenty brightly painted fan-cooled cottages (from US$320/260 in winter/summer) scattered above an impossibly turquoise bay and overlooking the Shekerley Hills. There's a beautiful pool, an aromatherapy/massage treatment room (for which you pay extra) and, while the inclusive food is not of the highest quality, there is a top-notch new restaurant on site called *Sheer* (see p.97), for which you also pay extra.

Cocos

Valley Road, Lignum Vitae Bay ☎460 2626, ℻462 9423, ⓦwww.cocoshotel.com. Another all-inclusive "get-away-from-it-all" spot ideal for couples. The fifteen rooms are very simply done (no TV, no phone and a mosquito net rather than air-conditioning), but each has beautiful views out over the ocean and across the broad crescent of Jolly Beach. There's good food, too, on the candlelit terrace below (see review, p.96). Room prices run from US$125/100 in winter/summer.

Curtain Bluff

Old Road ☎462 8400, ℻462 8409, ⓦwww.curtainbluff.com. For the seriously rich only – room prices start at a whopping US$850/495 a night in winter/summer – this is a spectacular all-inclusive hotel, built on the craggy bluff that overlooks Carlisle Bay and Cades Reef. The beautiful, spacious rooms all have a balcony or garden patio with a view of the ocean. Rates include all meals and drinks, scuba diving, sailing on the hotel's private yacht and a host of other top-class facilities.

Galley Bay

Five Islands ☎462 0302, ℻462 4551. Sprouting up between a bird-filled lagoon and a nearly mile-long stretch of beach, this resort is best suited for a romantic retreat. Indeed, none of the seventy rooms, which are mixed nearly evenly between individual thatched-roof cottages and wooden bungalows, are equipped with televisions or phones, though bathrobes and private patios are standard. A large lagoon-like pool and two fine restaurants round out the package. All-inclusive rates begin at around US$700 a night during high season.

Hawksbill Beach

Five Islands ☎462 0301, ℻462 1515, ⓦwww.hawksbill.com. Attractive all-inclusive hotel that sprawls over a vast area on the Five Islands peninsula, overlooking the bay and the jagged rock that pokes from the sea, giving the place its name. Four beaches, dramatic views, lovely landscaped gardens and a restored sugar mill (that's been converted into a store) all add to the atmosphere. There's a variety of accommodation options, from quiet beachfront cottages and club rooms to suites with balconies looking out towards Hawksbill Rock – prices start at US$300/265 in winter/summer.

Jolly Beach Resort

Lignum Vitae Bay ☎462 0061, ℻562 2302, ⓦwww.jollybeachresort.com. Vast all-inclusive resort – 480 typically small and rather unattractive rooms scattered along half a kilometre of good white beach – with four restaurants, seven bars, a disco, a small casino, tennis courts and free watersports (training and rental), including windsurfing, waterskiing, small sailboats and paddle boats. In a place this size, you can't avoid feeling part of a big crowd, and the food is nothing to write home about, but on the whole the place offers pretty decent value. All-inclusive rates per couple start at US$250/230 in winter/summer.

Jolly Harbour Villas

Jolly Harbour ☎462 7771, ℻462 7772, ⓦwww.jollyharbour-marina.com. Modern complex of about fifty waterfront villas, mostly two-bedroom with a full kitchen and a balcony overlooking the harbour. Plenty of shops, restaurants and sports facilities nearby (including a golf course and a large, communal swimming pool) plus a new casino and nightclub. Still, the place feels somewhat bland and unimaginative. Doubles start at US$190/140 in winter/summer.

Rex Blue Heron

Johnson's Point ☎462 8564, ℻462 8005, ⓦwww.rexcaribbean.com. Medium-sized and very popular all-inclusive on one of the best west-coast beaches, with 64 comfortable, brightly decorated rooms and a small pool just a stone's throw from the sea. All-inclusive rates start at US$320/260 in winter/summer.

Royal Antiguan

Deep Bay ☎462 3733, ⓕ462 3732.
At nine storeys, this massive and rather ugly place feels like a big-city business hotel accidentally plonked down in the middle of the Caribbean. That said, the facilities are excellent, particularly for tennis and watersports, the rooms are comfortable and the beach busy but pleasant. If you can get a decent rate as part of a package (look for something in the neighbourhood of US$130/95 a night in winter/summer) it's not a bad place to stay – if you can handle the crowd, that is.

Yepton Beach Resort

Deep Bay ☎462 2520, ⓕ462 3240, ⓦwww.yepton.com. Nothing flash, and not on Antigua's best beach, but a pleasantly landscaped and welcoming little resort, with its own supply of windsurfers and small sailboats, and the occasional bout of entertainment – live bands and the like – thrown in for the guests. The rooms are good sizes, most have a full kitchen and prices are reasonable, at US$150/110 a night in winter/summer.

Restaurants and bars

Castaways

Jolly Harbour ☎562 4445. Daily for lunch and dinner. Good beach bar and bistro on a nice if crowded strip of sand. Food is tapas-style (EC$15–25), while on Sundays there's a pig roast (EC$30). Occasional live music.

Chez Pascal

Galley Bay Hill, Five Islands ☎462 3232, ⓕ460 5730, ⓦwww.chezpascal.net, ⓔchez@candw.ag. Mon–Sat for lunch and dinner. Good French restaurant serving classy food in an intimate, cosy setting. Mouthwatering dishes include starters of garlic snails (EC$31) or chicken liver mousse (EC$29); mains of steamed grouper in *beurre blanc* (EC$74) or rack of lamb with Provençal herbs (EC$200 for two people); and desserts of profiteroles or *tarte tatin* (EC$24). It's well out of the way on the Five Islands peninsula, with attractive views over the area and out to sea. To get here, pass the *Galley Bay* hotel (see overleaf), take a right and then go right again up a steep hill.

Cocos

At the *Cocos* hotel, Valley Road, Lignum Vitae Bay ☎460 2626 or 460 9700, ⓔcocos@candw.ag. Daily for lunch and dinner. One of the most romantic spots on the island – a candlelit terrace overlooking a gorgeous west-coast bay – and the food's pretty good, too. Look for starters of pumpkin soup, conch fritters or crab cakes for EC$12–16, and main courses of baked tuna with red peppers or grouper fillet with lime for EC$42–45.

The Dogwatch Tavern

Jolly Harbour ☎462 6550. Restaurant open daily from 6pm. Bar open Mon–Fri 4pm–late, Sat & Sun 5pm–late. Right beside the marina, an English-style pub decorated with flags, pennants and sailing regalia. There are tables indoors and out, pool tables and dartboards, and an inexpensive outdoor snack bar and grill, with burgers for EC$20, hot dogs for EC$10, red snapper with peas and rice for EC$28 and an 8oz New York strip steak with fries for EC$45.

Indigo on the Beach

Carlisle Bay ☎484 0000. Daily for breakfast, lunch and dinner. Lively restaurant right by the beach at the new *Carlisle Bay Hotel*, serving top-quality grills, seafood, pizzas and salads (EC$25–50).

Melini's Ristorante and Pizzeria

Jolly Harbour ☎462 7695. Daily except Sat for breakfast, lunch and dinner. Sat dinner only. Popular open-air Italian eatery, in a lovely spot right by the marina. The standard menu has pizzas for EC$26–36, steaks for EC$80 and schnitzels for EC$45, while specials might be duck breast with mango pepper jelly and island greens at EC$45 or lemon pepper tilapia at EC$38.

OJ's Beach Bar

Crabbe Hill Beach ☎460 0184, ☎462 8651. Daily 10am–11pm. Simple beach bar and restaurant right on the water's edge between Darkwood Beach and Turner's Beach. The food is excellent – sandwiches and burgers for EC$15–25 and a house speciality of spice-coated red snapper for EC$40 – and the setting is wonderful: sand under your feet, the place festooned with fishing nets and carved driftwood (the fruit of the owner's passion

for beachcombing) and, on a clear day, a great view of the neighbouring island of Montserrat.

Peter's BBQ Steakhouse

Jolly Harbour ☎462 6026. Daily for breakfast, lunch and dinner. Heavily meat-oriented barbecue zone overlooking the marina, with reasonable if unspectacular offerings. There are daily lunch specials like barbecued chicken and chips or sandwiches for just EC$15; dinners of steaks, lamb or seafood kebabs with rice or veal in cream sauce for around EC$55; and an open salad bar for EC$26.

Sheer

At the *Cocobay Resort*, Ffryes Beach ☎562 2400. Tues–Sat 7pm–11pm.

▼ INDIGO ON THE BEACH

Wonderfully imaginative and eclectic food at this beautiful cliff-side restaurant, with only twelve tables and just one sitting. The menu, which fuses Asian and South American flavours, includes starters of duck terrine wrapped in seaweed, shrimp and tilapia ceviche and foie gras tortellini (EC$36–46), and mains of sugar cane tuna with cucumber and shrimp salsa, Bengali spiced rabbit and quail and pine nut- and mint-crusted lamb with black fig (EC$65–75). Save room for dessert: the ice cream alone is outstanding, with pumpkin seed flavour and a delicious Bailey's and hazelnut mix (EC$26).

Steely Bar

Jolly Harbour ☏462 6260. Daily 8am–late. Food is offered all day at this lively place, overlooking the marina in the heart of the Jolly Harbour complex, 250 metres along the boardwalk from *Melini's* (see overleaf). A full English or American breakfast costs EC$23, while an extensive lunch menu features various salads (EC$19–27), hot dogs and burgers (EC$20–25). Dinner options might include pan-fried duck breast (EC$52) or Cajun snapper with rice (EC$43). There's entertainment every night, as well (see "Nightlife", next column).

Turner's Beach Bar & Grill

Johnson's Point ☏462 9133. Daily 10am–9pm. Delightful little restaurant on another of the best west-coast beaches, a stone's throw from the *Blue Heron Hotel*. It's an unpretentious place, with plastic furniture right on the sand, but the cooking is good and the atmosphere mellow. The evening menu includes chicken

curry (US$11), grilled red snapper (US$14), shrimp in pineapple (US$15) and grilled lobster (US$22), as well as vegetable or chicken rotis (US$7). During the day, you'll find the same menu, but even if you're not particularly hungry, it's a great place to retreat from the beach for a snack and a beer. Worth calling ahead for a reservation at night.

Entertainment and nightlife

Grand Princess Casino

Jolly Harbour ☏562 9900, ☏562 8777, ⓦwww .grandprincessentertainment.com, ⓔinfo@grandprincessentertainment .com. Open Tues–Sun noon–late. Monstrous new development in the heart of the Jolly Harbour area, with a massive casino, three restaurants and often featuring live jazz.

Royal Antiguan

Five Islands ☏462 3733. Open nightly. No cover. Normally the liveliest spot on the Five Islands peninsula, this hotel (open to non-guests; see p.96) has a small disco and a casino area with pool tables, slots and video games.

Rush Nightclub

At the Grand Princess Casino, Jolly Harbour ☏562 7874. Wed–Sun 10.30pm–late. Cover EC$15. This new, nicely air-conditioned club has quickly become one of the most popular spots on the island for late-night partying. The music is a mix of Latin, disco, R&B, reggae and calypso, while the people getting down to it are a mix of young Antiguans and visitors to the island.

Steely Bar

Jolly Harbour ☎462 6260. Open nightly until late. No cover charge. The main all-around entertainment zone for the Jolly Harbour area, with large TVs showing sports matches, a steel band on Friday nights, karaoke on Saturday, movies on Sunday and always a crowd of people milling about. See opposite for a review of its kitchen.

Barbuda and Redonda

With its magnificent and often deserted beaches, its spectacular coral reefs and its rare colony of frigate birds, the nation's other inhabited island, **Barbuda** – 48km to the north of Antigua – is well worth a visit. Don't expect the same facilities as on Antigua; accommodation options are limited, you'll need to bring your own snorkelling or diving gear and you'll find that schedules – whether for taxis, boats or meals – tend to drift. This is all, of course, very much part of the island's attraction.

Barbuda is a throbbing metropolis, however, compared with Antigua's other "dependency", the tiny and now uninhabited volcanic rock known as **Redonda**, some 56km to the southwest in the main chain of the Lesser Antilles, between Nevis and Guadeloupe.

Getting there and getting around

The only scheduled **flights** to Barbuda are from Antigua on Carib Aviation (local ☎462 3147 or 462 3452, ℮caribav@candoo.com, UK ☎01895/450 710, ℮caribav@itgmarketing.co.uk, US ☎646/336-7600). Four flights leave daily from the main airport in Antigua (7am, 8am, 9am and 5pm, returning thirty minutes later in each case) and cost US$50 round-trip. The flight takes twenty minutes. More excitingly, the journey can be made by **boat**, although the cost of the 4hr crossing from St John's to River Landing on Barbuda's south coast tends to be pretty exorbitant, at around US$150 one-way. A handful of local boat operators run occasional trips (try Foster Hopkins on ☎460 0212 or Byron Askie on ☎460 0065) or you could ask around with the charter companies.

If you visit independently, **getting around** is likely to be your major headache. There is no bus service, and distances (and the heat) are sufficient to put all but the hardiest off the idea of walking anywhere. Also, you've no guarantee of finding one of the island's tiny **taxi** fleet in action, so it's worth calling ahead to try to **rent a car** from a private citizen: try Mr Burton (☎460 0103 or 460 0078), Mr Thomas (☎460 0015), Byron Askie (☎460 0065) or Junie Walker (☎460 0159), one of whom can usually oblige for around US$50 per day. Alternatively, ask around at the airport – there's usually a crowd there to meet the flights.

Taking a **day tour** to the island is the best way to guarantee getting both a driver and a boat operator to take you to the bird sanctuary (see p.102). Both D&J Tours (☎773 9766) and Jenny's Tours (☎461 9361) will organize a carefully packaged tour for US$160, including flights, pick-up at Barbuda's airport, a Jeep tour of the island, lunch and a boat visit to the bird sanctuary. Your driver will also leave you on the beach for as long as you want – just remember to take a bottle of water. Occasional day tours by boat are run by Adventure Antigua (☎727 3261, ⓦwww.adventureantigua.com) and Tropical Adventures (☎480 1225, ⓦwww.tropicalad.com), both of whom run to the Barbudan beaches for snorkelling, birding and beach cruising. The cost is around US$120 per person.

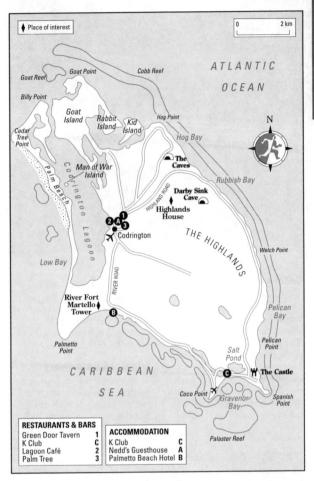

RESTAURANTS & BARS

Green Door Tavern	1
K Club	C
Lagoon Café	2
Palm Tree	3

ACCOMMODATION

K Club	C
Nedd's Guesthouse	A
Palmetto Beach Hotel	B

Codrington

Codrington, Barbuda's capital and only settlement, holds almost the entire population of 1500 people within its grid of narrow streets. It's a well spread-out place, with plenty of brightly painted single-storey clapboard or concrete buildings. There are a couple of guesthouses, as well as a handful of restaurants, bars and supermarkets, but, for the most part, people keep to themselves, and there is little sign of life apart from a few curious schoolchildren, dogs and the occasional goat. On Sundays the capital livens up with a cricket match at the Holy Trinity School.

▲ CODRINGTON

Codrington Lagoon

To the west of town, Codrington Lagoon is an expansive area of green, brackish water, fringed by mangroves. The lagoon is completely enclosed on its western side by the narrow but magnificent strip of Palm Beach (see opposite), but there is a narrow cut to the north where fishing boats can get out to the ocean. Lobsters breed in the lagoon and you'll probably see them at the pier being loaded for export to Antigua – an important contribution to the local economy.

Frigate bird sanctuary

To the northwest of Codrington Lagoon, a series of mangrove clumps known as Man of War Island serve as the home and

▼ CODRINGTON LAGOON

breeding ground for the largest group of frigate birds anywhere in the Caribbean.

You'll need a boat to get anywhere near these birds, motoring out to the edge of the shallows where they live and then poling the boat punt-like to their nests. The sight as you approach is quite spectacular – the mothers will take to the skies as you draw near, joining the multitude of birds wheeling above you, and leaving their babies standing imperiously on the nest but watching you closely out of the corner of their eyes. The display gets even more dramatic during the mating season, from late August to December, when hundreds of the males put on a grand show – puffing up their bright-red throat pouches as they soar through the air just a few metres above the females, watching admiringly from the bushes.

Small boats leave for the frigate bird sanctuary from the main pier just outside Codrington and charge around US$50 per boat. If you just turn up without notice, there is no guarantee that you'll find someone to take you out, so it's advisable to visit as part of a tour or to make arrangements through your hotel or car rental.

Palm Beach

West along Codrington Lagoon. On the west coast, on the far side of Codrington Lagoon (and so only really accessible by boat), gently curving Palm Beach offers 22km of dazzling white sand interspersed with long stretches of pink, created by the tiny fragments of millions of seashells washed up over the years. It's a great place to sunbathe, swim and snorkel, though there's little shade here – ask your boatman to drop you near one of the groves of casuarina trees; he'll come back for you a few hours later.

▼ PALM BEACH

Highlands House

North of Codrington, a series of dirt roads fan out across the upper part of Barbuda. One of these leads into the heart of the island, to the scant remains of Highlands House, the castle the first Codringtons built on the island in the seventeenth century. The home must have been pretty extensive, for the ruins – crumbling walls and the occasional piece of staircase – cover a wide area. The views across the island from here are as panoramic as you'll find.

The caves

On the northeastern side of the island (another dirt road leads up here), a series of caves have been naturally carved into the low cliffs. These are thought to have sheltered Taino and possibly Carib Indians in the centuries preceding the arrival of Europeans. However, scant evidence of their presence has been found here, except for some unusual petroglyphs.

The entrance to the main cave is opposite a large boulder, with the ruins of an old watchtower built up alongside. You'll need to scramble up the rocks for five minutes, then make a short, stooped walk inside the cave to reach the petroglyphs – a couple of barely distinguishable and very amateurish faces carved into the rockface. What is more noticeable is where pieces of rock have been prised away, a decade or so ago, by tourist vandals eager for their own chunk of ancient art. Alongside the petroglyphs, a large dome-shaped chamber – the "presidential suite" – was

▼ BARBUDAN CAVES

Shipwrecks around Barbuda

The shallows around Barbuda are littered with **shipwrecks**, the last resting place for some 150 vessels that failed to navigate safely through the island's dangerous coral reefs. Salvage from the wrecks was an important source of income for the islanders from at least 1695, when the *Santiago de Cullerin* ran aground with 13,000 pesos, destined for paying the garrisons on the Spanish Main in South America. During the following century, ships hitting the reefs included slavers, cargo ships and warships, with the Barbudans recovering everything from cases of brandy to dried codfish, sugar and coal. Income from salvage reached a peak of around £7000 a year by the early 1800s, though improved navigation techniques during the following century saw the number of wrecks decline sharply. To dive these wrecks, it's best to make arrangements with a dive shop on Antigua to bring over the necessary equipment by boat or plane (for dive shop listings, see "Sport and outdoor activities", p.119).

probably the main home of the Indians within the complex.

A couple of kilometres east of these caves, the **Darby Sink Cave** is one of hundreds of sinkholes on the island, dropping seventy feet to a mini-rainforest where palmetto palm trees, shrubs and birds proliferate. It's a steep climb down into the sinkhole, so you're probably best doing it with a local guide.

Rubbish and Hog bays

On the east coast, not far at all from where the caves are, the attractively named Rubbish Bay and Hog Bay are littered with driftwood and other detritus washed up by the Atlantic Ocean and offer great opportunities for beachcombing. At many other places around the island you'll spot tiny bays and coves where you can jump out of your car for a private swim and some snorkelling; Castle Bay, on the west coast, and White Bay, on the south coast near Palaster Reef, are particularly worth a look.

River Fort

In the southwest of the island, not far south of Codrington,

you can clamber around some substantial remains at the River Fort, just beyond a coconut grove near the *Palmetto Beach Hotel* (see review, p.107). The fort provides a surprisingly large defence for an island of Barbuda's size and importance. The island was attacked by Carib Indians in the 1680s and by the French navy in 1710, but there was too little valuable property here to tempt any further assailants into braving the dangerous surrounding reefs. As a result, the fort never saw any action, and its main role has been as a lookout and a landmark for ships approaching the island from the south.

The fort remains are dominated by a Martello tower, one of the many built throughout the British Empire during the Napoleonic Wars on the plan of a tower at Cape Mortella in Corsica – hence the name. Right below the tower, the River Landing is the main point for access to Barbuda by boat and is always busy with trucks stockpiling and loading sand onto barges to be taken to replenish beaches in Antigua – a controversial but lucrative industry for the Barbudans.

▲ SPANISH POINT

Spanish Point

East of the River Fort, the road leads out past the luxurious *K Club* hotel (see review, opposite) to the isolated Spanish Point, where a small finger of land divides the choppy waters of the Atlantic from the calm Caribbean Sea. Maps indicate a castle on Spanish Point, but if you make the effort to get here all you'll find are the ruins of a small lookout post. More interestingly, there is a marine reserve just offshore at Palaster Reef, where numerous shipwrecks have been located in the shallows amid the fabulous coral and abundant reef fish. You can swim to the edges of the reef from the beach, so don't forget your snorkelling or diving gear.

Redonda

The little island of Redonda – a two-kilometre hump of volcanic rock rising a sheer 300 metres from the sea – was spotted and named by Columbus in 1493, but subsequently ignored for nearly four centuries. During the 1860s, however, valuable phosphate was found in bird guano there, and Redonda was promptly annexed by Antigua. Mining operations were begun, producing around 4000 tons a year by the end of the century. However, output declined after World War I, the mining ceased and the island has been unoccupied – except by goats and seabirds – since 1930.

Almost surreally, though, Redonda is still claimed as an independent kingdom. In 1865 a Montserratian sea-trader named Matthew Shiell led an expedition to the island and staked his claim to it. His objections to Antigua's annexation of the island were ignored, but it didn't stop him from abdicating in favour of his novelist son in 1880; he in turn passed the fantasy throne to the English poet John Gawsworth, who took the title Juan III and appointed a number of his friends as nobles of the realm, including Dorothy L. Sayers, J.B. Priestley and Lawrence Durrell.

Today, a character who styles himself Leo V – actually a history teacher in London – claims to have inherited the kingdom, using his title to promote the literary works of his predecessors. However, at least one pretender to the throne argues that Gawsworth had abdicated in *his* favour during a night of heavy drinking at his local pub back in England.

Redonda is occasionally visited by yachtsmen – though with no sheltered anchorage, the landing is a difficult one – but there is no regular service to the island, nor anywhere to stay save a few ruined mining buildings when you get there.

Accommodation

K Club

Coco Point ☎460 0300, ℻460 0305, ⓦwww.kclubbarbuda.com. Closed June–Nov. Stunning Italian-owned and -designed place in the south of Barbuda, a celebrity home away from home with its own golf course and watersports facilities. The accommodation, priced at around US$1200 a room per night, mainly consists of beautiful white bungalows, each with a kitchen, seafront verandah and spired roof, well-distanced from one another and all directly on the beach.

Nedd's Guesthouse

Codrington ☎460 0059. Just a handful of comfortable and airy rooms, for roughly US$75 a night, with a kitchen and grocery store downstairs. If it's full, the owner should be able to direct you to someone who'll rent you a room.

Palmetto Beach Hotel

Palmetto Beach ☎460 0440, ℻462 0742, ⓦwww.palmettohotel.com. Smart hotel on a fantastic beach, with 24 beachfront suites, all with air-conditioning and a private verandah. The rooms (US$300/250 a night in winter/summer) are big, comfortable and stylishly decorated, while the chef is Italian and the food excellent – much of it (including the bread and pasta) is made fresh on the premises.

Restaurants and bars

Green Door Tavern

Codrington. Daily 11am–9pm. Good low-cost local food, such as pepperpot and conch stew (EC$25–35), with a barbecue on Friday and Saturday evenings and an easy-going vibe at all times.

K Club

At the *K Club* hotel, Coco Point ☎460 0300, ⓔkclub@candw.ag. Daily for lunch and dinner. Set on an exquisite beach, the *K Club* is beautifully designed and furnished in Italian-style white tile, columns and natural wicker. Except at busy times, anyone visiting the island is welcome for lunch and dinner – but you should still call to book ahead. Expect great Mediterranean-style food – freshly caught seafood is a speciality – beautiful people and hefty prices: the *prix fixe* menu is US$150 a head.

Lagoon Café

Codrington ☎460 0439. Daily for lunch and dinner. The main nightly hangout in Codrington, a dimly lit place offering simple meals like steamed grouper or curried chicken with peas and rice (EC$25–40), as well as guys playing dominoes and the (very) occasional live band.

Palm Tree

Codrington ☎460 0395. Daily for lunch. Good island food, particularly for fish and lobster (EC$30–50), but you'll need to let them know that you're coming (preferably a day in advance) and what you'd like to eat.

Essentials

Essentials

Arrival

All **flights** to Antigua touch down at V.C. Bird International Airport, on the island's north coast. There is **no bus service** from the airport, though there are numerous **car rental** outlets at the terminal. **Taxis** – arranged through the dispatch desk – cost around US$6 to Dickenson or Runaway bays, US$7 to St John's or US$25 to English Harbour.

If you arrive on Antigua by **cruise ship**, you'll dock at either Redcliffe or Heritage quay, in St John's (see p.38 for more on these two quays). From there, you can either take a taxi to anywhere on the island (see "By taxi", overleaf); a bus to English Harbour, Parham or Willikies (see "By bus", below); or rent a car (see "By car", overleaf).

Entry requirements

Citizens of Britain, Ireland, the US, Canada, Australia and New Zealand can enter Antigua without a **visa** and stay for up to six months. You will, however, need a **passport** (valid for at least six months after the date of onward travel) and a return ticket or proof of onward travel. You might also be asked to show that you have sufficient funds to cover your stay; if you can't satisfy the immigration authorities, they have the right to deny you entry. You will also be asked where you intend to stay, though your answer will not of course be binding.

Island transport

A lot of people come to Antigua, make straight for their hotel and spend the next fortnight lying on the beach. For those who want to tour around and see the island, though, there are a variety of options.

Speedy and inexpensive buses run to certain parts of the island, particularly between St John's and English Harbour on the west and south coasts, although none go to the big tourist area of Dickenson Bay and Runaway Bay. If you want to tour around, you're invariably better off renting a car for a couple of days. If you just want to make the odd excursion or short trip, hiring taxis can work out to be a better deal.

By bus

The public transport system in Antigua is patchy, with **buses** offering fast, frequent and inexpensive service between St John's and English Harbour, via the centre of the island, and less frequent service to Parham and Willikies on the east coast (from where it's a fifteen-minute walk to the Long Bay beach). There is no service to the tourist strip of Runaway Bay and Dickenson Bay on the northwest coast, nor to the airport. Buses and **minibuses** also run along the west coast between St John's and Old Road, stopping off beside several good beaches and the local hotels en route. They also run out to the Five Islands peninsula. For the south and west coasts, buses and minibuses use the West End bus terminal near the public market in St John's; for the east coast, they use the east terminal near the Rec (see pp.45 & 39, respectively).

Few of the buses run to any schedule, often departing only when they are reasonably full. Always ask the driver where he's going and tell him well in advance of where you want to get off. Stops are normally marked, though you'll find that the minivans will usually stop anywhere en route. Few buses run after dark or on Sundays.

By car

Antigua is an easy country to **drive** in; driving is on the left, the roads are mostly good and distances are small. True, signposting is abysmal, but it's hard to get seriously lost – asking passers-by is the best way to get information if you do. In St John's, though, the streets are narrow and poorly lit, so driving there at night is normally best avoided.

Rental prices start at around US$40 per day, $250 per week; third-party **insurance** is included in the price. If you don't have a credit card that offers free collision damage insurance, you'll have to pay another US$10–12 per day if you want to cover potential damage to the rental car.

When renting, you'll need to buy a local **driving licence** for US$20 (valid for three months) and to show a current licence from your home country or an international driver's licence. You'll also normally need a credit card to make a security deposit. Check the car fully to ensure that every dent, scratch or missing part is inventoried before you set off. When returning the car, don't forget to collect any credit-card deposit slip.

Reliable firms include Avis (☎462 2840), Budget (☎462 3009), Dollar (☎462 0362), Oakland (☎462 3021), Steads (☎462 9970) and Thrifty (☎462 9532). Each of these can provide you with a car at the airport or deliver one to your hotel.

By taxi

Finding a **taxi** in Antigua – identifiable from an "H" on their numberplates – is easy in St John's, Nelson's Dockyard or at the airport, but less straightforward in other areas of the island, where you'll often need to call (or ask your hotel to arrange) for one. Fares are regulated but there are no meters, so make sure that you agree on a price before you get into the car. At the airport there is a list of

government-approved rates: US$7 to St John's, US$6 to Dickenson Bay or Runaway Bay, US$25 to English Harbour. If you rent a taxi for a day's sightseeing, expect to pay around US$60–70. Two good taxi companies are West Bus Station Taxis (☎462 5190) and Antigua Reliable (☎460 5353).

Cycling and motorbikes

Since Antigua is so small, and there are few steep inclines, it is ideal **cycling** territory. Bikes can be rented for as little as US$15 per day, US$70 a week. Hiring a scooter or **motorbike** is just as fun – prices normally start at around US$35 per day, US$175 a week (plus US$20 for the local driving permit) – and can be a fantastic way of touring around, though you'll need to watch out for madcap drivers on the main roads. Rental agents for both bikes and motorbikes include Cycle Krazy, on St Mary's Street in St John's (☎462 9253), and Paradise Boat Sales at Jolly Harbour (☎460 7125).

Tours

If you fancy leaving the transportation to others, there are a couple of local companies who offer islandwide **sightseeing tours**, either to a set itinerary or customized to your desires. Remember to check whether the price includes entrance fees to the various attractions. Your hotel may also organize tours direct. If you can't get a good price from any of the companies listed below, you could check with some of the taxi operators (see "By taxi," above).

Tropikelly Trails (☎461 0383, ⓦwww.tropikellytrails.com) offer five- to six-hour tours from US$65 per person, including a picnic lunch, with trips to Great Fort George, Boggy Peak and a pineapple farm. Estate Safari jeep tours (☎463 4713) and Island Safari (☎562 5337, ⓦwww.tropicalad.com) offer similar tours, including Betty's Hope sugar plantation, Great Fort George and lunch on the beach. For **tours to Barbuda**, see the box on p.100.

Yachting charters

Charters – essentially, a private vacation on a fully crewed yacht – can be arranged through *Sunsail Club Colonna* (☎462 6263) or Nicholson's Yacht Charters (☎460 1530), both at English Harbour (though *Sunsail*'s hotel is actually on the north coast). Needless to say, this activity is only for the very wealthy.

Information and maps

Foreign branches of the **Antigua Tourist Office** (ATO) stock plenty of information on the country, including brochures on the main tourist attractions and upcoming events, and a good road map. Once you're in Antigua, you can get the same information from the ATO office in St John's (see p.38) or from their desk at the airport. Most of the car rental outlets will also provide you with a free map of the island when you rent from them.

Antigua has no dedicated listings magazine for music, theatre and other events, though the daily *Antigua Sun* newspaper carries regular arts and events details. Keep an eye also on flyers posted up around the island; local radio stations (see p.115) also advertise major events.

Antigua tourist offices overseas

Canada 60 St Clair Ave East, suite 304, Toronto, Ontario M4T IN5 ☎416/961-3085, ℻416/961-7218.

UK Antigua House, 15 Thayer St, London W1M 5LD ☎020/7486 7073, ℻020/7486 9970.

USA 610 5th Ave, suite 311, New York, NY 10020 ☎212/541-4117, ℻212/757-1607; 25 SE 2nd Ave, suite 300, Miami, FL 33131 ☎305/381-6762, ℻305/381-7908.

The ATO has no branches in Ireland, Australia or New Zealand.

Antigua on the Internet

As you'd expect, the island has plenty of websites dedicated to it, covering everything from hotels, restaurants and tour groups to online daily newspapers and government departments. Below you'll find a few of the more helpful general sites on offer.

Useful websites

Antigua and Barbuda Tourist Authority ⊛www.antigua-barbuda.org. The official site of the national tourism authority has information on upcoming events as well as offers on places to stay and car rental outfits, many of which you can book through the site.

Antigua Carnival ⊛www.antiguacarnival.com. The summer schedule is set out in detail, there's a "scrapbook" of last year's Carnival and details of this year's bands, some of whose songs you can download.

Antigua Nice ⊛www.antiguanice.com. Masses of information on the island, from hotel and restaurant reviews to details of travel agents and links to the island's latest news.

Cricket ⊛www.cricinfo.com. Somewhat surprisingly, given the importance of cricket on Antigua, no Antigua-specific cricket website exists. For now, the best way to find out information on matches is via this excellent, but generalized, site. The West Indies Cricket Board also has a good site, ⊛www.windiescricket.com.

Nick Maley's Island Arts ⊛www.antiguatoday.com/islandarts. Online information from Nick Maley, creator of *Star Wars*' Yoda, about his Island Arts business (see p.39 for more), plus helpful links to other informative Antigua-based sites.

Sailing Week ⊛www.sailingweek.com and www.antiguaclassics.com. Both sites are packed with information on the two weeks in April when Antigua's sailing tradition really comes into its own. See also the box on p.76.

Money and costs

Antigua is not a particularly cheap country to visit, and prices for many items are at least as much as you'd pay at home. Bargaining is generally frowned upon, but, particularly during the off-season of April to November, it can be worth asking for a reduced rate on items such as accommodation or car rental.

Currency

The island's unit of currency is the **Eastern Caribbean dollar** (EC$), divided into 100 cents. It comes in bills of $100, $50, $20, $10 and $5, as well as coins of $1, $0.50, $0.25, $0.10, $0.05 and $0.01. The rate of exchange is fixed at EC$2.70 to US$1 (giving you, at the time of writing, roughly EC$4.80 to UK£1), though you'll get a fraction less when you exchange money. In tourist-related business, the US$ is often used as an unofficial parallel currency, and you'll often find prices for hotels, restaurants and car rental quoted in US$ (a policy we have adopted in this guide). Bear in mind, though, that you can always insist on paying in EC$ (and the exchange rate usually works out slightly in your favour). If you are using US dollars or travellers' cheques to pay a bill, check in advance whether your change will be given in the same currency (it usually won't).

Costs

Accommodation will likely be the major expense of your stay, and most visitors pay this up front as part of a package. Double rooms can start as low as US$40/£22 a night for a simple room away from the beach. On the beach, the cheapest options clock in at US$100–150/£55–82 in high season (winter), or US$75–125/£41–68 in low season (summer). All-inclusives start in the neighborhood of US$200/£110 or so a night (many with a minimum-stay requirement), and only go up from there: the very exclusive *K Club* on Barbuda, for example, costs a whopping US$1200/£655 a night. Keep in mind, too,

that every place adds government tax of 8.5 percent onto the total bill, and that almost all add a service charge of 10 percent.

Aside from room costs, a realistic daily budget, including a decent meal out, the occasional taxi ride and a bit of evening entertainment, begins at about US$40/£25 – but really the sky's the limit.

Travellers' cheques, credit cards and banking hours

The safest method of carrying money is in the form of **travellers' cheques**. While sterling and other currencies are perfectly valid and accepted in the island's banks, US dollar travellers' cheques – due to the fixed rate between US and EC dollars – are the best ones to have. They are available for a small commission from most banks, and from branches of American Express and Thomas Cook; make sure you keep the purchase agreement and a record of cheque serial numbers safe and separate from the cheques themselves. Once in Antigua, the cheques can be cashed at banks (you'll need your passport or other photo ID to validate them) for a small charge.

Major credit cards – American Express, Visa, MasterCard – are widely accepted, but don't necessarily expect the smaller hotels and restaurants to take them. You can also use the cards to get cash advances at most banks, though you'll pay both commission to the bank and hefty interest to your credit card company. Also note that vendors will often try to add on five percent of the price of something if paid on a credit card.

Banking hours are generally Mon–Thurs 8am–3pm, Fri 8am–5pm; branches of the Antigua Commercial Bank are also open on Saturday from 9am to noon (see p.125 for locations). Many **hotels** will also exchange money, though if you're changing anything other than US$ the rate is usually a bit worse than the banks.

Wiring money

If you run out of money, and can't get it out of an ATM, you can have someone at home **wire you money**, via either Western Union (ⓦ www.westernunion.com) or Money-Gram (ⓦ www.emoneygram.com). Expect a charge of about US$15 to send US$100. You can pick up the money from any Western Union or MoneyGram agent on the island. Both companies have agents in St John's, Western Union on Old Parham Road (daily 8am–10pm; ☎463 0102) and MoneyGram at *Joe Mike's Hotel* (see p.47 for address and contact info).

Communications and the media

Antigua's **postal service** is reasonably efficient. The GPO in St John's is open Mon–Fri 8am–4pm (5pm Fri) and has poste restante (general delivery) facilities for receiving mail. There are also branches at the airport, at the Woods Centre and at English Harbour, and you can buy stamps and send mail at many of the hotels. **Postal rates** are reasonable: to the USA and Canada, air mail is EC$1.50, postcards EC$0.75; to the UK and Australasia, air mail is EC$1.80, postcards EC$0.90.

Calling within Antigua is simple – most hotels provide a **telephone** in each room (though be wary of surcharges). You'll also see **phone booths** all over the island, and these can be used for local and international calls. Most of the booths take phonecards only – they're available at hotels, post offices and some shops and supermarkets. If you want to use your **mobile phone**, it'll have to be set up for a US network (not likely if you're coming from Britain or Australasia) – and charges are likely to be high; you should check with your service provider before leaving home. For looking up phone numbers, hotel rooms and phone booths often have a **directory**; failing that, call directory assistance on ☎411. To reach the operator dial ☎0.

International calls

To phone Antigua from abroad, dial your international access code (UK ☎001, Ireland ☎001, Australia ☎0011, New Zealand ☎00; from the US or Canada, just dial ☎1) + 268 + seven-digit number.

To phone abroad from Antigua, dial the international access code (☎011 when calling the UK, Ireland, Australia, or New Zealand; unnecessary when calling the US or Canada), your country code (UK ☎44, Ireland ☎353, USA ☎1, Canada ☎1, Australia ☎61, New Zealand ☎64) + area code (minus first 0, if there is one) + number.

Newspapers and radio

As always, local newspapers and radio are a great way to find out what's on the nation's mind. The daily *Antigua Sun* is the best paper, concentrating on domestic news but with a decent section on news from the wider Caribbean and the rest of the world and, invariably, a big sports section. The main radio stations are the public service channel ABS (620 AM), and the commercial Sun FM (100.1 FM). They both carry news, sport, chat shows and music, mostly international hits with a sprinkling of local tunes.

Accommodation

Many visitors book their accommodation as part of a package deal, to get the best rates possible; you can be hooked up with an easy-going guesthouse, an apartment or a plusher resort, depending on your wants.

A significant and growing number of accommodation options are **all-inclusive** hotels. The simple concept behind these places is that you pay a single price that covers your room, all meals and, normally, all drinks and watersports. If you're thinking of booking an all-inclusive, focus on what you specifically want out of it. *Sandals* and the giant *Jolly Beach Resort*, for example, have several restaurants and bars, so you don't have to face the same menu every night, while smaller places like *Rex Blue Heron* offer less variety, but a bit more space on the beach (for reviews of these three places, see pp.56 & 95, respectively). Remember, too, that the allure of drinking seven types of "free"

cocktail in a night or stuffing your face at the "free" buffet quickly fades, especially if you want to get out and sample Antigua's great restaurants and bars.

A more positive trend is top-quality restaurants like *Chez Pascal* and *Harmony Hall* offering accommodation (for reviews of these two places, see pp.67 & 94, respectively). Some of the smaller, independent hotels on the island have also banded together in a venture called VIP, or Very Intimate Places. It's worth checking out their website (www.antigua-vip.com), which presents a range of options suitable to the type of trip you're taking.

Wherever we've listed accommodation, we've quoted **prices** for the least expensive double room during high season (mid-December to mid-April, aka winter) alongside, where applicable, prices for the least expensive double during low season (mid-April to mid-December, aka summer).

Food and drink

There are plenty of good eating options on Antigua and, though prices are generally on the high side, there's usually something to suit most budgets. Around most of the island, hotel and restaurant menus aimed at tourists tend to offer familiar variations on Euro-American-style food, shunning local specialities – a real shame, as the latter are invariably excellent and well worth trying if you get the chance. If you're heading to Barbuda, don't expect the same level of choice and sophistication as on Antigua. Away from the posh hotels, restaurants and bars are low-key and, like the island's pace of life, exceedingly slow.

Traditional Antiguan food

Almost everywhere, breakfast is based around coffee, cereal, toast and eggs, and

will usually include fresh fruit, one of the country's strong points. Expect to find paw-paws, bananas and the sweet Antiguan black pineapple year-round, while in season – generally between May and August – make a special effort to look out for the delicious local mangoes and sapodillas.

For other meals you'll find that **seafood** – as you'd expect – is one of the island's strong points. Of the fish, the tasty and versatile red snapper and grouper are the staples but, if you're lucky, you'll come across swordfish, mahi mahi and the very meaty marlin on the menu. Lobster is usually the priciest item, anywhere from EC$45–85 depending on season and the type of establishment. You'll also find conch (pronounced "konk") – a large shellfish often curried, stewed or battered in fritters, though best of all eaten raw in conch salad, when it's finely chopped with hot and sweet peppers, cucumber and lemon juice – as well as the giant local cockles and whelks, usually served in a buttery garlic sauce.

Other Antiguan specialities include the fabulous ducana (a solid hunk of grated sweet potato mixed with coconut and spices and steamed in a banana leaf); pepperpot stew, with salt beef, pumpkin and okra, often served with a cornmeal pudding known as fungi; goat or conch water (tender stewed goat or conch cooked with onions, butter, chives, thyme, cloves and browning, served with bread to mop up the gravy); various types of curry; salted codfish; and souse – cuts of pork marinated in lime juice, onions, hot and sweet peppers and spices.

Vegetarians will find their choices strictly limited – there are some great vegetables grown on Antigua, including pumpkins, okra and the squash-like christophene, but many menus don't include a single vegetarian dish, and even the widely available rice and peas often contains a piece of salted pork. Your best bet is probably to phone ahead and see if there are any true-blue veggie options; otherwise, opt for self-catering.

Drinking

For **drinking**, Wadadli is the local beer, a reasonable brew though not quite a match for the superb Red Stripe, a Jamaican beer brewed under licence on the island. Other regular beers on offer include Heineken, Guinness and the Trinidadian Carib. Rum is the most popular spirit, used as the basis for a range of cocktails from piña coladas to Cuba Libre (rum and Coke, with a twist of lime). The

English Harbour and Cavalier brands are both made on the island, though real aficionados of the stuff will want to look out for Mount Gay Extra Old from Barbados or the Haitian Barbancourt, both brilliant Caribbean rums, best served neat on ice.

As for **soft drinks**, you'll find the usual brands of sodas as well as the tasty sparkling grapefruit drink Ting, made locally, and a range of delicious local juices made from passion fruit, tamarind, guava and soursop. Look out, too, for vendors standing by piles of green coconuts; for a couple of EC dollars they'll cut the top off one for you to drink the sweet, delicious milk.

Restaurant costs and hours

If a service charge is not added to your bill, you should tip 10 to 15 percent. Opening hours are fairly standard – lunch typically from noon until 2 or 2.30pm, and dinner from 6pm. Bear in mind that many of the smaller restaurants close the kitchen early (around 9pm), particularly when business is slow. Additionally, some restaurants close for a couple of months over the summer, sometimes on a whim, depending on how quiet the season is expected to be.

During the winter season (Dec–April) it's worth making a reservation at many of the restaurants we've recommended; if you've got your heart set on a special place, you should probably arrange it a couple of days in advance. And finally, a word on **prices**: some restaurants quote their prices in EC$, others in US$, others in both. We've followed their practice, using whichever currency a particular restaurant quotes.

Ocean and beach safety

No shots are needed before heading to Antigua – the major tropical diseases were eradicated long ago – and you'll find that the only real threat to your physical

welfare is the intense **Caribbean sun**. Many visitors get badly sunburned on the first day and suffer for the rest of the trip – you'll see them peeling around the island. To avoid their fate, it's advisable to wear a strong sunscreen at all times; if you're after a tan, start strong and gradually reduce the factor. As for exposure times, 15 minutes a day in the early morning or late afternoon is recommended, if rarely followed; unreconstructed sun-worshippers should at least avoid the heat of the day between 11.30am and 2.30pm. For the sunburned, aloe vera gel is available at the island's pharmacies (see "Directory", p.125, for a list of these).

While you're on the beach, steer clear of the **manchineel trees**, recognizable by their shiny green leaves and the small, crab apple-like fruits scattered around on the ground. The fruit is poisonous and, when it rains, the bark gives off a poisonous sap that will cause blisters if it drips on you. The sea, too, poses a handful of threats. Don't worry about the rarely seen sharks or barracudas, which won't spoil your visit, but watch out for spiny black **sea urchins**. They're easily missed if you're walking over a patch of sea grass; if you step on one and can't get the spines out, you'll need medical help. Jellyfish too are best avoided. Finally, mosquitoes and tiny sandflies can be an occasional problem, particularly on the beach in late afternoon; take **insect repellent** to keep them at bay.

Sport and outdoor activities

The confirmed beach addict and the watersports fanatic are equally at home in Antigua, with a variety of great beaches to choose from and plenty of operators offering excellent diving, snorkelling, waterskiing and other activities. Also on the water, a number of companies offer trips along the coast by boat or catamaran, and you can charter boats for deep-sea fishing. There are plenty of land-based options, too, with a couple of good golf courses, a horse-riding stable and hiking, mountain-biking and jeep trips.

Although diving options around Antigua are best in the south, the northwest coast is probably the best spot for general watersports; **Dickenson Bay** in particular has several reputable operators at its northern end. The sea is pretty calm here year-round and, beyond the protected swimming zone, you can waterski, windsurf, parasail or jet-ski. **Paradise Reef**, a half-kilometre-long coral garden to the north of the bay, is a popular spot for glass-bottom boat trips and snorkelling, and there are good coralheads offshore around tiny **Prickly Pear Island**, a short boat-ride to the northeast.

Barbuda surpasses even Antigua in the quality (and remoteness) of its beaches, and its snorkelling and diving opportunities are also world-class. Unfortunately, the island has little in the way of infrastructure to support tourists looking for watersports – meaning you may have to take your own gear.

Diving and snorkelling

Diving is excellent on the coral reefs around Antigua and Barbuda, with most of the good sites – places like Sunken Rock and Cape Shirley – on the south side of the larger island. Many of these sites are very close to shore, rarely more than a fifteen-minute boat ride away. Expect to see a wealth of fabulously colourful reef fish, including parrot fish, angelfish, wrasse and barracuda, as well as the occasional harmless nurse shark and, if you're lucky, dolphins and turtles. The reefs for the most part are still in pristine, unspoiled condition and, though there is no wall diving and most dives are fairly shallow, there are some good cliffs and canyons and a handful of wrecks.

Antigua has plenty of quality dive operators scattered conveniently around the island, so you should always be able to find a boat going out from near where you're staying. Rates are pretty uniform: reckon on around US$75 for a single-tank dive, US$100 for a two-tank dive and US$90 for a night dive. Beginners can get a feel for diving by taking a half-day resort course, which covers basic theory and includes a shallow-water (or pool) demonstration and a single dive. The course costs around US$100, and allows you to continue to dive with the people who taught you, though not with any other operator (as you're not really certified). Full open-water certification – involving theory, tests, training dives and four full dives – is rather more variable in price, costing US$400–500, depending on the time of year and how busy the operator is. Call around for the best deal.

Serious divers should consider a **package deal**, either involving a simple three or five two-tank dive package (ie, three or five separate trips, consisting of two dives each; roughly US$200–300 and US$350–450, respectively) or a deal that includes accommodation and diving. Prices for these can be pretty good value, particularly outside the winter season. It's worth contacting the dive operators directly to find out the latest offers.

Barbuda's diving is at least as good as Antigua's, with countless wrecks dotted around the nearby reefs (see p.105 for more on Barbuda's shipwrecks). Sadly, though, at the time of writing there is no established dive outfit on the island. You can ask some of the Antiguan dive operators for the latest information, or check with one of the agencies that offers tours to the island – they can normally arrange for certified divers to be provided with tanks and guides on Barbuda, though the costs can be hefty.

Snorkelling around the islands is excellent, too, and several of the dive operators take snorkellers on their dive trips,

mooring near some good, relatively shallow coralheads. Reckon on around US$20–25 for an outing, including equipment. That said, a boat ride is far from essential for snorkellers – there are loads of good spots just a short swim offshore from both Antigua and Barbuda, and these are mentioned throughout the Guide. Most of the top hotels have snorkelling gear for hire or loan, but if you're not at one of these, finding the equipment can be tricky (try Deep Bay Divers in St John's; see below); it's worth bringing a mask and fins with you, certainly if you're heading to Barbuda.

Dive operators

Aquanauts At the *St James Club* hotel, Mamora Bay ☏460 5000. Good, professional south coast outfit with top-quality equipment, catering to the hotel guests and drop-ins from elsewhere.

Deep Bay Divers Redcliffe Quay, St John's ☏463 8000, ⊛www.deepbaydivers.com. New outfit with a 34ft dive boat with room for up to fourteen divers and offering trips down to Cades Reef in the southwest (a fifty-minute ride), Ariadne Shoal (also fifty minutes away but much further offshore) or straight out to Sandy Island, fifteen minutes' west of St John's. Snorkellers welcome if there's room; snorkelling gear costs US$15 to rent.

Dive Antigua At the *Rex Halcyon Cove* hotel, Dickenson Bay ☏462 3483, ☐462 7787, ⊛www.diveantigua.com. Based on the northwest coast, Dive Antigua is the longest-established and best-known dive operation on the island; prices are normally a little higher than most of the other operators. They also offer a glass-bottomed boat to take snorkellers out to the reef.

Dockyard Divers Nelson's Dockyard ☏460 1178, ☐460 1179. Decent-sized dive shop (and the only outfit in the English Harbour area offering snorkelling tours) that lays on diving trips around the south and west coasts.

Jolly Dive Jolly Harbour Marina ☏462 8305, ⊛www.jollydive.com. Second-oldest dive shop in Antigua and very popular with guests at the big, local hotels; look elsewhere if you want to go out in a small group.

Ultramarine At the *Sunsail Club Colonna* resort, Hodges Bay ☏462 6263. Good dive shop, though some distance from the best sites to the south. As well as regular dive trips, they also offer "surface scuba" for children under 12, who aren't old enough to go to any depth.

Boats and catamarans

There is no shortage of boat and catamaran trips to be made around Antigua, with the emphasis on being part of a big crowd all having a fun time together – not, it must be said, everyone's cup of tea. Most of the cruises charge a single price, including a meal and all the drinks you want, and the two main cruise companies, Kokomo and Wadadli Cats, offer virtually identical trips, travelling on large, comfortable catamarans.

The most popular cruise – a great way to see the island – sails right around Antigua, taking in some snorkelling and lunch at Green Island off the east coast. There is also a superb snorkelling trip to Cades Reef on the south coast, stopping off for lunch on one of the west-coast beaches, and another to uninhabited Great Bird Island – where there's plenty of bird life – off the northeast. Finally, there's a "triple destination" cruise on Sundays to English Harbour via Green Island, ending with a taxi ride up to the steel band party on Shirley Heights and another taxi home.

Each of these trips is offered by Kokomo and Wadadli, and both will pick up passengers from a number of different locations on the west coast. All are out from around 9am until 4pm, apart from the triple-destination tour, which runs roughly 10am to sunset. The circumnavigation cruise costs US$85 per person, Cades Reef US$70, and the triple-destination cruise US$100, all prices including snorkelling gear, a buffet lunch and an open bar. Tickets for children under 12 are half-price.

Cruise and boat tour operators

Adventure Antigua ☎727 3261 or 560 4672, ⓦwww.adventureantigua.com. Owner Eli Fuller takes passengers by smallish motorboat on a seven-hour eco-tour of the northeast coast of the island,

showing where the endangered hawksbill turtles lay their eggs, and through the mangrove swamps, looking out for rays, frigate birds, osprey and turtles. There are several snorkelling opportunities, and the guide lays on fresh fruit juices, rum punch and lunch on a deserted beach. Cost is US$90 per person, and the trip goes out between two and five times a week, depending on demand.

Excellence and Tiami ☎480 1225, ⓦwww.tropicalad.com. On sleek, luxurious new catamarans, trips around the island or to Cades Reef, Great Bird Island or Barbuda. Costs from US$85 per person.

Jolly Roger Pirate Cruises ☎480 1225, ⓦwww.tropicalad.com. Hearty party cruises, with rope-swinging and walking the plank for those piratically inclined and limbo competitions and calypso dance classes for the rest. Around US$60 per person.

Jabberwocky ☎775 0595 or 773 3115, ⓦwww.adventurecaribbean.com. Tailor-made cruises on a luxurious day-charter yacht. Pick whichever beaches and coves you want to visit around the island or even go overnight to Barbuda. Costs from US$85 per person.

Kokomo Cats ☎462 7245, ⓦwww.kokomocat.com. 'Round the island trips (Tues, Thurs, Sat, US$85), Cades Reef (Wed, US$70), Great Bird Island (Fri, US$70), and a quadruple-destination cruise (no different from a triple-destination cruise; Sun, $100) on speedy, well-appointed catamarans. Kokomo also offer sunset cruises on Thursdays from Jolly Harbour on the west coast, out from 4.30pm (US$40).

"Paddles" Kayak & Snorkel Club ☎463 1944, ⓦwww.antiguapaddles.com. Based in the village of Seatons on the northeast coast, this outfit offers half-day ecotours of mangroves, reefs and the local coast via motor boat, kayak, snorkelling and a nature walk.

Wadadli Cats ☎462 4792, ⓦwww.wadadlicats.com. Circumnavigation cruises (Thurs, Sat, US$85), Cades Reef (Wed, US$70), Great Bird Island (Fri, US$70), a sunset cruise (Sat, US$40), and a triple-destination cruise (Sun, US$100).

Sailing

Antigua is one of the prime sailing destinations in the Caribbean and, particularly during Sailing Week in April, the island becomes a refuelling and party stop for crowds of hearty yachters. If you're after some crewing on boats sailing between the West Indian islands, ask around and look out for crew notices at Nelson's Dockyard on the south coast and at the yacht charter outfits (Sun Charters and Nicholson's) just outside the dockyard. For information on Sailing Week and the preceding classic yacht regatta, see the box on p.76 and check out ⓦwww.sailingweek.com and ⓦwww.antiguaclassics.com.

Fishing

Various charter boats offer deep-sea fishing trips where you can go after wahoo, tuna, barracuda, snook, tarpon, bone fish and, if you're lucky, marlin and other sailfish. Prices for up to six people start at around US$400 for a half-day, $600 for a whole day, including rods, bait, food, drink and transport from your hotel. If you want to go on your own, operators will put you with another group if they can and charge around US$100 for a half-day.

Regular operators include Missa Ferdie (☎462 1440 or 460 1503, ⓔshoulj @candw.ag), Nightwing (☎460 5337, ⓦwww.fishantigua.com, ⓔace@candw .ag), Overdraft (☎462 1961 or 464 4954, ⓦwww.antiguafishing.com, ⓔnunesb@ candw.ag) and Phill's Eco Fishing (☎723 4303, ⓔfish@actol.net). If you hunt around at dockside, particularly in St John's and Jolly Harbour, you can find plenty of others.

If you just want to go out with some local fishermen – which can be an amazing experience – ask around at one of the main fishing settlements like Old Road on the south coast. Many will be grateful for an extra pair of hands, though you'll need to clarify in advance exactly what's expected of you – pulling lobster pots and fishing nets is extremely tough work and you may be at it for hours.

Other watersports

Many of the hotels have their own wind-surfers which you can borrow for no extra cost, and there's a windsurfing school (daily 9am–5pm) at Sunsail Club Colonna (see p.68) on the northeast coast. Non-guests can buy a day's watersports pass for US$100, or US$55 for a half (both allow you to attend the windsurfing school).

A little further east and not far from the airport, Dutchman's Bay is another good spot for windsurfing, whether you're a beginner or an expert. H2O Antigua (☎562 3933 or 728 2998, ⓦwww .h2oantigua.com) rents equipment for US$60 a day, with lessons starting at US$50.

On Dickenson Bay, Tony's Water Sports (☎462 6326), Sea Sports (☎462 3355) and Pop's (☎460 5644) offer a variety of watersports. A ten-minute **parasail** costs US$45, a similar period of **waterskiing** costs US$25, while **jet-skis** cost US$30 for half an hour (US$40 for a two-seater). If you want to do a lot of watersports, consider buying a day-pass for around US$50 from Sandals (see p.56). You'll also find various men offering you use of their jet-skis and small sailboats at negotiable prices; it usually works out cheaper than going with an established company – but bear in mind that insurance will be nonexistent.

Lastly, at Jabberwock Beach on the north coast, you can try the new sport of **kiteboarding** with an outfit called KiteAntigua (☎727 3983, ⓦwww .kiteantigua.com) – see p.60 for more information.

Golf

There are two eighteen-hole public golf courses in Antigua. Barbuda has a tiny course at the K Club, but it is open only to guests.

Golf courses

Cedar Valley Golf Club 5km north of St John's ☎462 0161, ⓕ562 2762, ⓦwww .cedarvalleygolf.ag, ⓔcedarvalley@candw .ag. A 6157-yard, par 70 championship course, and venue for the annual Antigua Open, held each November. It's a lovely course, lined with palms, flamboyants and cedars and, from its higher points, offers great panoramic views of the island. Given the dryness of the islands, water hazards are mercifully few but, that aside, it's a reasonably challenging course. Greens fees are US$35–45 in low/high season for eighteen holes (US$18–23 for nine holes), plus US$15–20 per person for rental of clubs and another US$30 if you want to rent a cart (US$15 for nine holes). The dress code is pretty relaxed, but you will need a collared shirt.

Jolly Harbour Golf Course 8km south of St John's ☎480 6950, 🌐www .jollyharbourantigua.com/golf.html. The island's other major golf location, a 6001-yard, par 71 course designed by American Karl Litten. It's an excellent course, flatter than Cedar Valley but (with seven lakes) more fraught with peril. Around US$50 for eighteen holes.

Horseback riding

Though you may well be offered a horse-back tour during your visit (often on a rather mangy and forlorn creature), there is only one official horse-riding stable on the island, located just west of Falmouth at Spring Hill (☎460 7787 or 460 1333). They have around a dozen horses and offer lessons for EC$50/US$20 per hour or simple riding tours of the area for EC$40/US$16 per hour.

Tennis and squash

Many hotels on Antigua have their own tennis courts, best at places like the *Royal Antiguan*, *Rex Halcyon Cove* and the *St James Club*, but there are a hand-ful of public tennis and squash courts available around the island, charging around EC$35/US$14 per hour, and EC$10/US$4 for hire of equipment.

Tennis and squash courts

BBR Sportive Jolly Harbour ☎462 6260. Private squash and four floodlit tennis courts at this west coast resort; rackets and other equipment can be hired.

Temo Sports English Harbour ☎463 6376. Two glass-backed squash courts and two floodlit synthetic-grass tennis courts, with all equipment available for hire. There's also a new burger bar and a good bar area with pool and darts. Round-robin

tennis tournament on Fridays; closed Saturday evenings and Sundays.

Cycling

Cycling is a great way of seeing Antigua, not least because there are few hills and – away from St John's – not much traffic either. Operators offer guided island tours by mountain bike, particularly through attractive places like Fig Tree Drive in the south; if you want to go it alone, several outfits will be happy to rent you a bike sans guide.

Cycle companies

Cycle Krazy St John's ☎462 9253. Group tours organized with a "support jeep" carrying drinks and first-aid gear. Around US$30 per person for a half-day tour, to many of the same places as Tropikelly Trails (see below).

H2O Antigua Dutchman's Bay, Coolidge ☎562 3933 or 728 2998, 🌐www .h2oantigua.com. Mountain bikes can be rented from this windsurfing centre for US$35 for a day, US$105 for a week.

Paradise Boat Sales Jolly Harbour ☎460 7125, 🌐www.paradiseboats.com. Bikes rented for US$15 per day, US$70 for a week.

Tropikelly Trails Fitches Creek ☎461 0383, 🌐 www.tropikellytrails.com. Impressively well-organized tour operator, whose popular guided bike tours – for example, down along the coast to Darkwood Beach, or up through the hills around Fig Tree Drive – start from St John's and cost US$35 a head including bike, helmet and drinks.

Hiking

There are plenty of great hikes in Antigua, a number of them described throughout the Guide. For US$20–35 per person, and assuming they can raise enough hikers to make it worthwhile, Tropikelly Trails (☎461 0383, 🌐www.tropikellytrails.com) runs a pleasant, moderately strenuous two-hour guided hike in the hills of the southwest. More elaborate and longer hikes are periodically organized by Peter Todd of the Hiking Company (☎460 1151) – call to find out what he has planned.

Jeep tours

Tropikelly Trails (☎461 0383, ⓦwww.tropikellytrails.com) and Island Safari (☎562 5337, ⓦwww.tropicalad.com) both offer great off-road tours, exploring both the human and natural history of Antigua. Island Safari does a nice combination package with a jeep tour in the morning, lunch on a deserted beach and a kayaking and snorkelling trip in the afternoon. These tours will each run you about US$85.

Helicopter tours

If you want to splash out, Caribbean Helicopters (☎460 5900, ⓦwww.caribbeanhelicopters.net) offer sightseeing tours for US$75 per person (15min, half-island tour) or US$130 (30min, full-island tour). Though expensive, it's a great way to see all of Antigua at once – 100 miles of shoreline, plus every beach, reef, hotel, and fort, all from an unrivalled bird's-eye view.

Crime and personal safety

Compared to what you'll encounter in Jamaica or several other Caribbean islands, **harassment** in Antigua is extremely mild. The itinerant vendors who patrol some of the beaches are the main culprits – you'll occasionally be offered drugs or pressed to look at some uninspiring crafts – but on the whole police crackdowns have kept them at a distance. If you're not interested, just be firm in saying no thanks and they'll leave you alone.

Violent **crime** involving tourists is rare but not unheard of. After dark, it's advisable to steer clear of unlit or unpatrolled areas of the beach, and you'll probably want to avoid the rougher areas of St John's, though there's no reason why you'd want to visit them. **Drugs** present an increasing problem on the island, particularly a growing use of crack cocaine, which is leading to a rise in theft and burglary to finance the habit. Marijuana use is just as widespread – and equally illegal – often distributed on the beaches, particularly on the south coast, to likely-looking punters. If you want it, you can get it, but bear in mind that there are plenty of undercover police around, and the local press runs stories daily of tourists facing heavy fines for possession.

Travelling with children

Calm, clear seas, shelving beaches, no serious health risks and a welcoming attitude make Antigua an ideal destination for babies, toddlers and children. Most hotels welcome families and give substantial discounts for children – those under 12 often stay free in their parents' room – but it's worth checking in advance whether they put any restrictions on kids, especially if you're heading for an all-inclusive; *Sandals*, for example, only accepts couples.

You may also want to check on babysitting/childminding facilities. The most child-friendly places like *Sunsail Club Colonna* (see p.68) have wonderful daytime crèches and clubs that kids of all ages can be dropped in and out of and feature a range of activities including sailing. One or two others like *Long Bay Hotel* (see p.67) have games rooms and sports equipment like sailboats and kayaks that will keep older children entertained for hours in a safe environment.

Festivals and events

The main events in Antigua are the summertime **Carnival** and April's Sailing Week, but there are various other events to distract you from the beach, including international **cricket**, **tennis** and **warri** (a board game) tournaments. The local and overseas tourist boards (see p.113) have full details of all the activities.

Annual events

January
Official start of West Indian cricket season ☎ 462 9090, ⊛ www
.windiescricket.com.

February
Valentine's Day Regatta Jolly Harbour ☎ 461 6324. A two-day event consisting of four yacht classes and seven short races.

March–April
Test cricket ☎ 462 9090, ⊛ www
.cricinfo.com and www.windiescricket.com.

April
Classic Yacht Regatta ☎ 460 1799, ⊛ www.antiguaclassics.com.

Sailing Week ☎ 462 8872, ⊛ www
.sailingweek.com. See box p.76.

May
Pro-Am Tennis Classic At the *Curtain Bluff Hotel* ☎ 462 8400, ⊛ www.curtainbluff.com
/sports.html.

July/August
Carnival ☎ 462 4707, ⊛ www
.antiguacarnival.com. See box p.40.

September
Bridge Championship ☎ 462 1459. Regional championship open to both locals and visitors.

October
National Warri Championship ☎ 462 6317. National competition for this ancient game that aficionados rank alongside chess, bridge and backgammon.

November
Antiguan Craft Fair At Harmony Hall ☎ 460 4120, ⊛ www.harmonyhall.com
/gallery.htm. A great opportunity to view local and regional arts and crafts. See also p.66.

Public holidays

New Year's Day	Jan 1
Good Friday	Fri before Easter Sunday
Easter Monday	day after Easter Sunday
Labour Day	first Mon in May
Whit Monday	end of May (varies)
Caricom Day	July 5
Carnival	first Mon and Tues in Aug
United Nations Day	first Mon in Oct
Independence Day	Nov 1
Christmas Day	Dec 25
Boxing Day	Dec 26

December
Nicholson's Annual Charter Yacht Show ☎ 460 1530, 🖱 www .nicholsonyachts.com/yachtshow. The world's oldest charter yacht show sees boats from all over the world converge on English Harbour and Falmouth – from sloops and cutters to schooners and catamarans, plus big power craft.

Directory

Unless otherwise stated, all services listed are in St John's.

Airlines American Airlines ☎ 462 0950; British Airways ☎ 462 0876; BWIA T480 2942; Carib Aviation ☎ 462 3147; Caribbean Star ☎ 480 2591; LIAT ☎ 480 5600; Virgin ☎ 560 2079.

Airport departure tax For international flights the departure tax is presently US$20 (EC$50), payable at the airport when you leave.

Ambulance Emergency ☎ 911 or 999, otherwise ☎ 462 0251.

American Express Corner of Long St and Thames St ☎ 462 4788, Mon–Thurs 8.30am–4.30pm, Fri 8.30am–5pm.

Banks St John's: Antigua Commercial Bank, St Mary's St at Thames St (Mon–Thurs 8am–2pm, Fri 8am–5pm); Bank of Antigua, Thames St at High St (Mon–Thurs 8am–3pm, Fri 8am–4pm, Sat 8am–1pm); Barclays, cnr of High and Market streets (Mon–Thurs 8am–2pm, Fri 8am–4pm); ABIB, Woods Centre (Mon–Thurs 9am–3pm, Fri 9am–4pm, Sat 9am–1pm). Nelson's Dockyard: Bank of Antigua (just inside entrance of dockyard; Mon–Thurs 8am–3pm, Fri 8am–4pm, Sat 8am–1pm).

Dentists Antigua Barbuda Dental Group, Newgate St ☎ 460 3368; Dr Maxwell Francis, Cross St at Newgate St ☎ 462 0058; Dr SenGupta, Woods Centre ☎ 462 9312.

Electric current The island standard is 110 volts with two-pin sockets, though a few of the older hotels still use 220 volts. Take adapters for essential items; some upmarket hotels and guesthouses have them, but you shouldn't count on it.

Embassies Canadian warden, St John's ☎ 462 1210; British High Commission, 11 Old Parham Road, St John's ☎ 462 0008; US Consular Office, Pigeon Point, English Harbour ☎ 463 6531. There is no Australian, Irish, or New Zealand embassy or commission in Antigua.

Film and photography equipment Island Photo, at the corner of Redcliffe and Market streets, sells film and does one-hour photo development; Benjie's, on Heritage Quay, offers the same service and has various camera accessories at duty-free prices.

Fire department ☎ 462 0044.

Hospitals St John's has the 225-bed public Holberton Hospital (☎ 462 0251) as well as the brand-new Mount St John's Medical Centre; both are on Queen Elizabeth Highway. Smaller health centres and clinics are distributed around the island.

Internet access There is an Internet café beside the customs office in Nelson's Dockyard and another just outside the dockyard (beside the supermarket next to *The Last Lemming*); access is also available at Parcel Post, Redcliffe Quay, St John's. Expect to pay EC$6 for 15 minutes.

Laundry Jolly Harbour: Burton's ☎ 462 7754; Nelson's Dockyard: near the dockyard café, no phone, daily 8am–4pm; St John's: Burton's, Independence Drive ☎ 462 4268.

Pharmacies Full service pharmacies in St John's: Benjies, Redcliffe St at Market St ☎ 462 0733 (Mon–Thurs 8am–8pm, Fri 8am–6pm, Sat 7am–9pm, Sun 9am–1pm), and Woods, Woods Centre ☎ 462 9287 (Mon–Sat 9am–10pm, Sun 11am–6pm). Jolly Harbour: Sysco (Mon–Sat 9am–5.30pm, Sun 11am–4pm).

Police The main police station is on Newgate St ☎ 462 0045. For emergencies call ☎ 462 0125 or ☎ 999 or 911.

Post office English Harbour: Mon–Fri 8.30am–4pm; St John's: Long St Mon–Fri 8.15am–4pm; Woods Centre Mon–Thurs 8.30am–4pm, Fri 8.30am–5pm.

Supermarkets English Harbour: Malones, near *Abracadabra*, daily 8am–5pm; Falmouth: C.E. Bailey, opposite *Harbour View Apartments*, daily 9am–6pm; Falmouth Harbour: Yacht Club Marina, daily 8am–6pm; Jolly Harbour: Epicurean, daily 8am–8pm; St John's: Epicurean, Woods Centre, daily 8am–9pm.

Taxis West Bus Station Taxis ☎462 5190; Antigua Reliable ☎460 5353.

Travel agents English Harbour: Nicholson's, on the approach to Nelson's Dockyard ☎562 2065 (Mon–Sat 9am–4pm); St John's: Bryson's, Long St at Thames St ☎480 1230 (Mon–Fri 8am–4pm, Sat 8am–noon).

ROUGH GUIDES
TRAVEL SERIES

THE ROUGH GUIDE TO
The Baltic States
Estonia, Latvia & Lithuania

THE ROUGH GUIDE TO
China

THE ROUGH GUIDE TO
Florida

THE ROUGH GUIDE TO
South America

THE ROUGH GUIDE TO
Sweden

THE ROUGH GUIDE TO
USA

THE ROUGH GUIDE TO
Vietnam

THE ROUGH GUIDE TO
Vancouver
With Victoria, Whistler and the Sunshine Coast

THE ROUGH GUIDE TO
The Philippines

Travel guides to more than 250 destinations from Alaska to Zimbabwe
smooth travel

ROUGH GUIDES TRAVEL...

ROUGH GUIDES

Rough Guides are available from good bookstores worldwide. New titles are published every month. Check www.roughguides.com for the latest news.

...MUSIC & REFERENCE

Also! More than 120 Rough Guide music CDs are available from all good book and record stores. Listen in at www.worldmusic.net

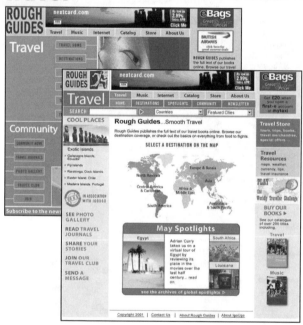

ROUGH GUIDE MAPS

Printed on waterproof and rip-proof Polyart™ paper, offering an unbeatable combination of practicality, clarity of design and amazing value.

CITY MAPS

Amsterdam · Athens · Barcelona · Berlin · Boston · Chicago
Brussels · Dublin · Florence & Siena · Frankfurt · London
Lisbon · Los Angeles · Madrid · Marrakesh · Miami
New York · Paris · Prague · Rome · San Francisco · Toronto
Venice · Washington DC and more...

COUNTRY & REGIONAL MAPS

Algarve · Andalucía · Argentina · Australia · Baja California
Brittany · Crete · Croatia · Cuba · Cyprus · Czech Republic
Dominican Republic · Dubai & UAE Egypt · Greece
Guatemala & Belize · Hong Kong · Iceland · Ireland · Kenya
Mexico · Morocco · New Zealand · Northern Spain · Peru
Portugal · Sicily · South Africa · South India · Sri Lanka
Tenerife · Thailand · Trinidad & Tobago · Tuscany
Yucatán Peninsula and more...

ROUGH GUIDES
REFERENCE SERIES

"The Rough Guides are near-perfect reference works"
Phililedphia Enquirer

History · Internet · Music
Restaurants · Football · Formula 1
Weather · Astronomy · Health
Movies · Videogaming · TV

DON'T JUST TRAVEL!

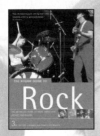

SMALL PRINT

A Rough Guide to Rough Guides

Antigua DIRECTIONS is published by Rough Guides. The first *Rough Guide to Greece*, published in 1982, was a student scheme that became a publishing phenomenon. The immediate success of the book – with numerous reprints and a Thomas Cook prize shortlisting – spawned a series that rapidly covered dozens of destinations. Rough Guides had a ready market among low-budget backpackers, but soon also acquired a much broader and older readership that relished Rough Guides' wit and inquisitiveness as much as their enthusiastic, critical approach. Everyone wants value for money, but not at any price. Rough Guides soon began supplementing the "rougher" information about hostels and low-budget listings with the kind of detail on restaurants and quality hotels that independent-minded visitors on any budget might expect, whether on business in New York or trekking in Thailand. These days the guides offer recommendations from shoestring to luxury and a large number of destinations around the globe, including almost every country in the Americas and Europe, more than half of Africa and most of Asia and Australasia. Rough Guides now publish:

- Travel guides to more than 200 worldwide destinations
- Dictionary phrasebooks to 22 major languages
- Maps printed on rip-proof and waterproof Polyart™ paper
- Music guides running the gamut from Opera to Elvis
- Reference books on topics as diverse as the Weather and Shakespeare
- World Music CDs in association with World Music Network

Visit **www.roughguides.com** to see our latest publications.

Publishing information

This 1st edition published August 2004 by **Rough Guides Ltd**, 80 Strand, London WC2R 0RL. 345 Hudson St, 4th Floor, New York, NY 10014, USA.

Distributed by the Penguin Group
Penguin Books Ltd, 80 Strand, London WC2R 0RL
Penguin Group (USA), 375 Hudson St, NY 10014, USA
Penguin Group (Australia), 487 Maroondah Highway, PO Box 257, Ringwood, Victoria 3134, Australia
Penguin Group (Canada), 10 Alcorn Avenue, Toronto, Ontario, Canada M4V 1E4
Penguin Group (NZ), 182–190 Wairau Road, Auckland 10, New Zealand
Typeset in Bembo and Helvetica to an original design by Henry Iles.
Printed and bound in Italy by Graphicom

144pp includes index
A catalogue record for this book is available from the British Library

ISBN 1-84353-319-7

The publishers and authors have done their best to ensure the accuracy and currency of all the information in **Antigua DIRECTIONS**; however, they can accept no responsibility for any loss, injury, or inconvenience sustained by any traveller as a result of information or advice contained in the guide.

1 3 5 7 9 8 6 4 2

Help us update

We've gone to a lot of effort to ensure that the first edition of **Antigua DIRECTIONS** is accurate and up-to-date. However, things change – places get "discovered", opening hours are notoriously fickle, restaurants and rooms raise prices or lower standards. If you feel we've got it wrong or left something out, we'd like to know, and if you can remember the address, the price, the time, the phone number, so much the better.

We'll credit all contributions, and send a copy of the next edition (or any other DIRECTIONS guide or Rough Guide if you prefer) for the best letters. Everyone who writes to us and isn't already a subscriber will receive a copy of our full-colour thrice-yearly newsletter. Please mark letters: "Antigua DIRECTIONS Update" and send to: Rough Guides, 80 Strand, London WC2R 0RL, or Rough Guides, 4th Floor, 345 Hudson St, New York, NY 10014. Or send an email to mail@roughguides.com

Have your questions answered and tell others about your trip at www.roughguides.atinfopop.com

Rough Guide credits

Text editor: Hunter Slaton
Layout: Dan May & Andy Hilliard
Photography: Ian Cumming
Cartography: Rajesh Chhibber, Animesh Pathak, Jai Prakash Mishra, Katie Lloyd-Jones, Miles Irving

Picture editor: Mark Thomas
Proofreader: David Price
Production: Julia Bovis
Design: Henry Iles
Cover art direction: Louise Boulton

SMALL PRINT

The author

Adam Vaitilingam is the author of many books on the Caribbean. He lives in Devon.

Romesh Vaitilingam is a writer and media consultant. An occasional travel writer, he more typically writes books and articles on economics, public policy and investment, including *The Financial Times Guide to Using the Financial Pages*, now in its fourth edition.

Acknowledgements

Romesh would like to thank Annemarie, Cara, Marco and super-nanny Claire Moore.

The editor would like to thank Romesh, Ian Cumming, Dan May, Andy Hilliard, Katie Lloyd-Jones, Miles Irving, the Delhi cartography team, Mark Thomas, Louise Boulton, David Price, and Andrew Rosenberg.

Index

Map entries are marked in colour

INDEX

DIRECTIONS on Screen

Put the guide on your computer or PDA

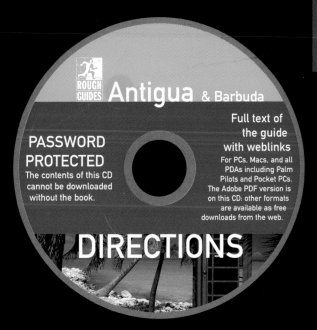

ROUGH GUIDES **Antigua** & Barbuda

PASSWORD PROTECTED
The contents of this CD cannot be downloaded without the book.

Full text of the guide with weblinks

For PCs, Macs, and all PDAs including Palm Pilots and Pocket PCs. The Adobe PDF version is on this CD: other formats are available as free downloads from the web.

DIRECTIONS

This CD contains the complete
Antigua & Barbuda DIRECTIONS
in Adobe PDF format, complete with maps and
illustrations. PDFs are readable on any
Windows or Mac-OS computer (including laptops).
The mini-CD also contains instructions for further free
downloads formatted for Pocket PC and Palm.

Insert the mini-CD in the central recess of any tray-loading CD-Rom drive: full instructions supplied. Note: mini-CDs will not work in slot-loading drives. Slot-loading drive owners or DIRECTIONS purchasers who have mislaid their mini-CD should go to www.directionsguides.com to download files as required. Note on platforms: Adobe supports maps and illustrations and is compatible with Mac and PC operating systems. Pocket PC and Palm platforms support text only.

www.roughguides.com

havaianas.

the best rubber sandals of the world

Available from:

Selfridges

Office

House of Fraser

Size

Urban Outfitters

Schuh

USC

JD Sports

www.office.co.uk

www.havaianas.com